# LEGENDARY GUITARS

# LEGENDARY GUITARS

JULIEN BITOUN

PHOTOGRAPHY BY ELEANOR JANE

CASSELL

1960 Gibson Les Paul Standard 'Rosie'

# 100 Legendary Guitars

**The book you are reading contains one hundred of the rarest, most sought-after and significant guitars, whose sound and history have shaped legends and continue to haunt the dreams of the most demanding musicians and obsessive collectors.**

•

It does not claim to be complete, however. It is not a history of the guitar from 1833 to the present day, and readers will notice the absence of a particular make or model. The hundred guitars that did make the cut will take you on a journey through the most important models, providing the perfect excuse to revisit the creators who have pushed the instrument to new limits, alongside anecdotes that make the history more human.

The selection of photos in Eleanor Jane's abundant archive also determined the choice of guitars. A photographer who has specialized in this subject for some 15 years, she has cast her lens over every major collection, every auction and every artist's backline, capturing it all from a very personal perspective. It is these photos that make this book the most beautiful collection of guitars ever assembled, rather than simply an assortment of generic snaps.

Each entry gives the date of manufacture and a history of the instrument shown in the photo, along with a song on which it can be heard and an estimated market value. This last is in constant flux, especially at the moment, so take it not as gospel but rather as an approximation, a ballpark figure. The suggested listening may be a title where the sound helped to define the model in question or, in some cases, a piece by the artist who owns the actual guitar. Again, this is a wholly subjective choice and not the equivalent of a 'ten guitar sounds to hear before you die' list.

I advise you to browse through this book in the same way as it was written: in no particular order, pausing at the photos that catch your eye. This is also why we have elected not to classify the guitars in any way other than to create an aesthetically pleasing book.

Welcome to this review of the most beautiful guitars in history, and remember one key thing: a musical instrument is only as good as the notes it lets you play. Happy reading!

# CONTENTS

PLEASE!
DO IT
MY WAY

# Gretsch
# White Penguin

**There are rare guitars and then there's the White Penguin, a model whose existence could not even be confirmed until a vintage example eventually turned up. The White Penguin has become the white whale for those collectors with pockets deep enough to hunt it.**

•

t can be tricky to get a handle on the Gretsch range, not least because most o the company's guitars have both a name and a model number ('White Falcon and '6136', for example). The specifications of the guitars tend to evolve ove ime, too, with no very obvious break points.

Among all its models, 6134 is a particularly mysterious designation. The numbe ocates it between two solid-body Corvettes for beginners (the single-pickup 6133 and the twin-pickup 6135), but the White Penguin is the most high-end o all Gretsch's semi-solid-body models. It is in fact a Duo Jet gussied up as a White Falcon (white finish with gold hardware and binding), in much the same way as the 6121 was a Jet-style take on the Chet Atkins 6120 (the 'Big Orange').

Jnlike the 6121, however, there were so few examples of the White Penguin in existence that for a long time it was no more than a rumour among connoisseurs A maximum of 30 or so had supposedly been manufactured between 1956 and 1962, but it did not even feature in contemporary catalogues, appearing only in a price list reserved for resellers in 1959. One White Penguin surfaced n the 1980s, confirming the existence of this white whale, but very few vintage examples have turned up since. About 15 of this single-cutaway version with Filter'Tron humbuckers were made, and this particular one belonging to David Gilmour sold at auction for nearly half a million US dollars in 2019. Penguins don't come cheap.

Year of manufacture: 1958
Country: United States
Approximate resale value: £125,200
Hear it on: The White Stripes, 'Icky Thump' (2007)
Guitarist: Jack White

GRETSCH

# Suhr
## Pete Thorn

**Suhr is the archetypal boutique brand, a business with no interest in becoming big enough to compete with the major players, but keen to offer the best possible instruments whatever the price point. Nowadays, Suhr is a proper factory with dozens of employees, but the brand has retained its human scale.**

•

The term 'boutique' derives simply from the fact that this type of instrument was originally made directly in the shop where it was to be sold. The boutique market has never been bigger or more dynamic than it is today, whether for pedals, amplifiers or guitars.

John Suhr is no beginner, however. He learned the ropes in the 1970s, repairing guitars in Rudy Pensa's store on New York City's famous 48th Street, before launching the Pensa-Suhr brand. The company combined Pensa's designs and Suhr's luthier skills, and the resulting guitars became the tools of choice for a certain Mark Knopfler, no less. Suhr went on to work at Custom Audio Electronics (an amplifier and rack system brand) in the 1990s before joining the Fender Custom Shop in 1995. He finally set up shop on his own in California in 1997, and now manufactures very high-end guitars, amplifiers and pedals.

The guitar shown here is the signature model for Pete Thorn, a musician with a long track record as sideman for such superstars as Chris Cornell and Melissa Etheridge. He is also very prolific as a guitarist on video channels and social networks, testing lots of equipment, and he has a very precise notion of what he expects from an instrument. The model shown here is the Suhr Pete Thorn Standard, a version with twin humbuckers (designed specially for Thorn by Suhr) and a hybrid Fender/Gibson construction with a mahogany body and a bolt-on neck in the same wood.

Everything about this guitar exudes respect for a job well done, creating an instrument that aims to be the ultimate means of expression for versatile and demanding musicians.

Year of manufacture: 2020
Country: United States
Approximate resale value: £2,500
Hear it on: Pete Thorn, 'Into Focus' (2018)

# Gibson Flying V

**The Flying V is now one of those guitars that is considered 'standard'. Despite its daring configuration, its shape has become part of the furniture to such an extent that it features in countless logos and visual designs. But this has not always been the case – far from it.**

•

By 1965 the Kinks had become one of the most important groups of the British Invasion thanks to 'You Really Got Me', their hit of the previous year. When they touched down in New York in June for their first American tour, the airline had mislaid their lead guitarist Dave Davies's guitar, so he set about locating an emergency replacement. He found nothing to his taste among the guitars on display in the shop, but when the salesman brought out a dusty case containing a guitar that had been mouldering in the stockroom for seven years, he fell head over heels in love with both its look and its sound. Davies became the musician who brought the Flying V to the attention of the general public, showcasing a model of which only about a hundred examples had been made in 1958 and 1959 before production was halted owing to its lack of success.

Other players (such as Lonnie Mack and Albert King) had discovered its virtues before Davies, but the Kinks had a much larger audience. Gibson even decided to resume production of the model in 1966, making a version in mahogany (rather than korina) that would be used by Jimi Hendrix and Marc Bolan in particular. Nonetheless, the Flying V remained an 'odd' guitar, an instrument that never enjoyed any real popular success despite its use by a host of guitarists of stature, including Michael Schenker, Neil Young, Andy Powell of Wishbone Ash, Kirk Hammett from Metallica, Webb Wilder, Tom Petty and Mike Campbell.

The original korina Flying V has now become a priceless collector's item, but only the most eccentric guitarist would dare to include it in their collection. Its shape has, however, inspired numerous more or less spiky and asymmetrical versions in the meantime, notably the Jackson used by the guitarist Randy Rhoads that has since become a go-to in the world of metal. It's a nice bit of payback for a model no one would touch with a ten-foot pole in 1958.

Year of manufacture: 1958
Country: United States
Approximate resale value: £500,700
Hear it on: The Kinks, 'Till the End of the Day' (1965)
Guitarist: Dave Davies

# Gibson
## ES-330

**Despite an uncanny resemblance to its elder sibling the ES-335, the ES-330 is a beast of an entirely different stripe. In fact, the instrument has a lot more in common with the big jazz archtops of the preceding decades.**

•

The model numbers for the ES-330 are officially ES-330T (for this version with an oddly located central single pickup) and ES-330TD for the twin-pickup model (D standing for double, presumably). The T means thinline, which locates this guitar within the line of models launched in 1955 as quarter-body versions of the brand's traditional archtops. The Byrdland (a double signature model for Billy Byrd and Hank Garland), the ES-350T and the ES-225T were the first three models to feature a much shallower body for easier handling.

The ES guitars released at the end of the 1950s are thus part of this line, but with a difference in size; the ES-335, 345 and 355 all have a central maple block in the body that means they are semi-hollow, while the ES-330 is completely empty inside. Although its two rounded horns might give it a superficially similar appearance, this difference in structure ensures a radically different sound and playing feel.

Overall, the ES-330 is a less high-end model than the 335; the 335 has humbuckers rather than P90s (and does not even exist in a single-pickup version), and it also features the crown inlay on the headstock that the 330 is lacking. Most importantly, however, the 335 neck meets the body at the nineteenth fret rather than the 330's sixteenth, making the latter's neck shorter, with access to the higher frets that is nothing to write home about. At a time when solos were beginning to become the default option in a song, and with a hollow-body's sensitivity to feedback, such choices prevented it from finding its niche.

It was the Epiphone version of this model, the famous Casino, that was to become legendary in the hands of the Beatles. John Lennon certainly seemed to manage well enough with three fewer frets.

Year of manufacture: 1960
Country: United States
Approximate resale value: £4,200
Hear it on: Big Star, 'In the Street' (1972)
Guitarist: Chris Bell

DRIVE
BRIGHT
IN
OUT
BRIGHT
OPERATE
ON
INDICATOR
STANDBY
OFF

# Charvel
## San Dimas Style 1

**The Charvel superstrat was the 1980s guitar par excellence and could be seen in the hands of every poodle-haired, spandex-clad rock star of the period. The brand has nonetheless managed to update its image and is now one of the most conspicuous stars in the metal galaxy, in addition to all the nostalgia it evokes.**

•

The brand's story begins with the man who gave it its name, Wayne Charvel. He worked at Fender in the 1970s before opening his own repair shop, fixing faults but also doing modifications using parts that he made himself. His company failed to thrive, however, and in 1978, after declaring bankruptcy, he sold it to the luthier Grover Jackson.

Jackson set about producing bodies and necks as aftermarket parts, followed by entire Strat-style guitars of eye-catching appearance, and in 1980 the virtuoso guitarist Randy Rhoads (who had just joined Ozzy Osbourne's group) worked with him to create an aggressively styled V-shaped model. For fear that the radical aspects of this guitar might taint Charvel's reputation, he put his own name on the headstock, and that is how Charvel and Jackson became two competitors originally owned by the same luthier.

After a host of organizational changes, the two brands were ultimately bought up by Fender in 2002. Since then a new generation of shredders, metal riff-merchants and fusion guitarists have plumped for Charvel, in particular Guthrie Govan, Joe Duplantier (Gojira) and Jim Root (Slipknot).

The full designation of the model shown here is the Pro-Mod San Dimas Style 1 HSS FR M; Style 1 means a Strat-style body (with Style 2 being Tele-shaped), while HSS refers to the classic configuration of a humbucker in the bridge position with two single coils for the widest possible sonic palette. The Floyd Rose (FR) is unmistakably the vibrato first released in the 1970s that revolutionized pitch-bending, and if you're not playing at lightning speed after all that, you're obviously not trying hard enough.

Year of manufacture: 2021
Country: Mexico
Approximate resale value: £600
Hear it on: Ozzy Osbourne, 'Bark at the Moon' (1983)
Guitarist: Jake E Lee

Seymour Duncan
Seymour Duncan

# Fender
## Telecaster Custom Colour

**Because of its rather stripped-down shape and design, you might think the Telecaster is destined to symbolize nothing more than the utilitarian side of the guitar, a highly effective blunt instrument with which to make music. No one would dwell on the beauty of a screwdriver, admittedly, but it would be a crying shame to pass over a vintage Candy Apple Red Tele without admiring it appropriately.**

•

It must be said that vintage Telecasters in custom colours are anything but two a penny. Fender had begun offering all its models in a range of 14 custom colours at the very beginning of the 1960s, but at a mark-up, and far fewer Telecasters than Stratocasters would be manufactured once the latter became the brand's star model (particularly after Jimi Hendrix had begun opening up its horizons in 1967). In addition, the price premium for a custom colour made little sense for a Telecaster, which had found its niche at a lower price point than the other models in the range.

For all these reasons, custom colour Telecasters are very much a rarity on the vintage market, and the one shown here is a very nice example in Candy Apple Red. This finish was taken from the world of automobiles, but, unlike other Fender finishes of the era, it was not a paint advertised in the General Motors catalogue. This colour was developed by an artist from Kustom Kulture, a movement that modified cars to give them a unique appearance, just like the sleek, shiny lustre of Candy Apple Red (with the entirely appropriate initials CAR).

Candy Apple Red replaced Shell Pink among Fender's custom colours in 1963 and was so successful that six more metallic finishes were added in 1965. In 1963 the red was applied on top of an undercoat of silver; that was switched to gold in 1966, resulting in a darker shade of CAR, as can be admired on this incomparable Telecaster.

Year of manufacture: 1968
Country: United States
Approximate resale value: £16,700
Hear it on: Rick Nelson, 'I Got a Woman' (1963)
Guitarist: James Burton

Amp
FENDER ELECT. INST. CO.
FENDER
PAT.NO.

**Fender Telecaster, 1968**
Incorporating the pickup in the metal bridge plate is one of the elements that gives the Fender Telecaster its particular sound. On this model from 1968, the bridge saddles are threaded steel rather than the brass of older versions. In addition, the ageing of nitrocellulose lacquer produces an instantly recognizable 'checking' that luthiers at the Custom Shop are still striving to reproduce.

# 5150 Series Standard

**Few guitarists have had an impact that can compare with that of Eddie Van Halen at the turn of the 1980s. The Dutchman defined how musicians would sound and play for the next 15 years, and we are still in his debt, not to mention that the music made by his group continues to strike a chord almost 50 years later.**

•

When the first Van Halen album came out, in 1978, no one had ever heard anything like it, and the entire world stopped to listen. Besides his incredible technique and the fluidity and fire of his playing, Eddie Van Halen flummoxed guitarists with his astonishing sound, which he achieved with relatively simple equipment. Brands immediately tried to emulate his formula by copying the guitar he had built himself, the famed Frankenstrat.

The 1980s thus became the decade of the superstrat – Stratocaster-shaped guitars with a humbucker in the bridge position and a Floyd Rose vibrato, based on the Van Halen model. Eddie finally agreed to work with Kramer's marketing department in 1983 and went on to assemble a replica of his Frankenstrat with parts sourced from the New Jersey brand, a task made all the easier because the neck of the original Frankenstrat was already a Kramer.

Van Halen moved over to Ernie Ball/Music Man in 1991, followed by Peavey in 1992, before finally launching his own brand in collaboration with Fender in 2005, calling it simply EVH. Since then, every guitar of Van Halen's career has been reproduced in replica at EVH, and the brand continues to exist despite the death of the great man himself in 2020. This 5150 Standard model has been assigned the guitarist's favourite number (it was also the name of his studio). It is strongly inspired by the Kramer models he used, with a 'banana' headstock, a Floyd Rose (with a D-Tuna device to retune to drop D), a killswitch button and, most importantly, this incredible neon-pink finish that is impossible to ignore.

Year of manufacture: 2021
Country: Mexico
Approximate resale value: £500
Hear it on: Van Halen, 'Panama' (1984)
Guitarist: Eddie Van Halen

# Gibson
# 1960 Les Paul Standard

**The third and final year of the famous Burst's existence was the one in which its specifications changed the most, but a Les Paul Standard from 1960 remains one of the most desirable and expensive guitars in the world of vintage electrics, especially when there is an interesting story behind it.**

•

The year 1960 marked the end of production of the Les Paul Standard in this format before Gibson switched to the double cutaway shape that later became known as the SG. It was also the year of the slim taper neck, which became radically thinner; of controls that were swapped out for reflector knobs; and, most importantly, of a change in the composition of the red paint. This last innovation might seem trivial, but the sunburst Les Paul Standards of preceding years had tended to lose their red upon exposure to UV light, giving rise to uniformly yellow finishes like the famous lemon burst. The change in red undertaken in 1960 resulted in a more vivid hue that did not fade over time.

When you buy a Burst, however, you are mainly purchasing its history and provenance. There are so many questionable and fake instruments in circulation (contemporary Gold Tops 'converted' to Bursts, for example) that a collector will be more relaxed about investing in a guitar whose previous ownership is known.

The holy grail in such situations is therefore a 'one owner' Burst, that is to say an instrument resold directly by the person (now necessarily rather advanced in years) who bought it at the time. The guitar will ideally be accompanied by the invoice and the contemporary 'case candy', all the promotional paperwork that came with it from the shop in 1960.

This superb 1960 was the property of a single musician, Roselynn 'Rosie' Coleman, who was playing it in her group the Rhythmettes at the turn of the 1960s. The guitar was left in the basement for half a century, after which it resurfaced in mint condition, an almost priceless jewel.

Year of manufacture: 1960
Country: United States
Approximate resale value: £250,400
Hear it on: Eagles, 'Life in the Fast Lane' (1976)
Guitarist: Joe Walsh

Gibson
RHYTHM
TREBLE

# Dobro Angelus

**Dobro guitars are now so much a part of the resonator guitar market that they have become synonymous with it. People tend to call a resonator guitar of whatever brand 'a Dobro' with much the same lazy language that allows any paper tissue to be called 'a kleenex'.**

•

The Dobro story begins with National, a brand established in 1927 by the steel guitarist George Beauchamp (who also helped to develop the first electric lap steels with Rickenbacker) and the luthier John Dopyera. They had developed a guitar design with a metal resonator body integrating three cones to achieve the best possible sound projection.

Dopyera left the company the following year to found Dobro with four of his brothers. Dobro is in fact a contraction of Dopyera Brothers and, by lucky chance, also means 'good' in the Dopyeras' native Slovakian. The Dobro design made use of the resonator principle, but with only a single cone and a wooden body. Dobros were therefore more powerful (which was the reason the design had originally been invented) and less expensive to produce, a concern that was anything but trivial at a time when the Great Depression was putting musicians in a tight spot.

The instrument became the symbol of Delta blues guitarists, among them Son House and Bukka White. These musicians prized the volume the resonator brought them, which proved highly practical for being heard in a crowded bar where people had come to drink rather than listen to music.

Faced with the ubiquity of the electric guitar after World War II, the Dobro eventually fell into disuse, but fans of the blues never forgot it entirely. It underwent a considerable revival during the 1970s (with the rediscovery of American folk music) and in the 1980s, thanks to the original soundtrack recorded by Ry Cooder for the film *Paris, Texas* (1984), in which acoustic slide guitar creates a haunting atmosphere.

Year of manufacture: 1933
Country: United States
Approximate resale value: £3,300
Hear it on: Son House, 'Death Letter Blues' (1965)

GODIN LGT #1
ITEM 4
ITHL

# Wandré
## Brigitte Bardot

**There are two kinds of guitarist: those who have never heard of Wandré and those who dream of owning one. This Italian manufacturer did not last long and produced only a handful of instruments, but the lucky few musicians and collectors who have managed to track one down are unanimous in their verdict that these guitars exert a unique fascination to this day.**

•

There are, of course, those people who are prepared to pay over the odds for Silvertones and Airlines because of their fun and decorative aspects. But these prices are left in the dust by Wandré, whose guitars have been commanding sums more like the big American brands since the 2000s.

Antonio Vandrè Pioli was the son of a cabinetmaker and luthier. Having tried his hand at various jobs, he finally launched his own range of guitar models in 1957 (at the age of 31) and, after this proved a great success, opened a factory in Cavriago in northern Italy in 1958. All the Wandré guitars made over the next ten years came from this circular building. Very few European manufacturers were taking much interest in the electric guitar at the time, and Pioli took advantage of the instrument's novelty to indulge himself in every excess, both visual and technical.

Wandré guitars look absolutely unique to this day, an improbable mishmash of Art Deco and Surrealism with a touch of 1960s kitsch, such as the boob-shaped sound hole of this B B (Brigitte Bardot) model, named in honour of the actress. Wandré had his own ideas from a technical perspective, too, using an aluminium neck (a technique that would be adopted by other brands) running through the body to the bridge, a headstock that could be easily swapped out (either a slotted or a solid version), and rather particular hardware, from a distinctly improbable bridge to pickups made by Davoli, an Italian amplifier brand.

By the end of the 1960s Wandré had been left behind by a guitar market that was becoming a race to the bottom for the cheapest manufacturing possible, and it shuttered its factory. After several decades of almost total obscurity, however, an increasing number of musicians have been discovering the merits of this very particular brand.

Years of manufacture: 1960s
Country: Italy
Approximate resale value: £8,300
Hear it on: Robert Plant, 'Falling in Love Again' (2010)
Guitarist: Buddy Miller

HONOLULU

# Gretsch Corvette

**The Gretsch brand has always been renowned for its superbly designed, outsize hollow-body guitars, but it also dipped a toe into solid bodies. Its success there was a mixed bag, with the exception of the legendary Duo Jet, but its designs were immediately recognizable and always appealing.**

•

There are many links between the worlds of cars and of electric guitars, even stretching to the names of models (Fender's Jaguar and Mustang) and brands (Duesenberg). Gretsch has never held back in this respect, and the Brooklyn brand dipped into the Chevrolet catalogue to name the Corvette, its solid-body model for beginners.

Despite its rather late appearance in 1961, the Corvette was in fact Gretsch's first true solid-body, since the firm's electric model, the Duo Jet and its derivatives, actually had semi-hollow architecture. The Corvette was built on the same principles as the Les Paul Junior, with a simple mahogany body, a glued-in mahogany neck with a rosewood fretboard, and one or two pickups, depending on the model. With the 6132 and 6133 (like the one shown here), the Corvette was fitted with a single-bridge pickup; the 6135 featured a pair of HiLo'Trons, a Gretsch single-coil pickup model launched around this time and known for its very low output (which is why many Corvette owners have swapped such pickups for more powerful models). The vibrato was sourced from Burns – an odd choice when you consider that this is a British brand.

The two asymmetrical, pointed horns, chamfered body and red colour are more than a little reminiscent of the SG launched by Gibson very shortly before it. The Corvette failed to achieve the cult status of its competitor, however, and was relegated to the ranks of vintage oddities, albeit one with exciting tales to tell.

Years of manufacture: early 1960s
Country: United States
Approximate resale value: £1,300
Hear it on: Ida Mae, 'American Cars' (2023)
Guitarist: Chris Turpin

SCH SOU
M STICK
RUMS
GRETSCH
BURNS

# Fender
## Custom Shop Telecaster Thinline

**These days, the Fender Custom Shop mainly specializes in reproducing historical instruments. Vintage is too expensive, so musicians make do with these superb replicas. However, this workshop within a workshop – which styles itself the Dream Factory – is also perfectly capable of bringing the most harebrained, outlandish idea to life.**

•

The renowned relics sell like hot cakes and are almost exclusively Stratocasters and Telecasters, most often in sunburst or butterscotch, although sometimes in rarer but still historically correct custom colours (Tyler Bryant's shell-pink Strat, for instance).

When the Custom Shop opened its doors in 1987, however, it was first and foremost a place of creativity, an island of avant-garde R&D and a means for artists to achieve their wildest dreams. The first guitar to be officially manufactured under the Custom Shop banner was in fact a Stratocaster/Esquire double-neck.

It is now rare for the Custom Shop to offer truly outlandish designs, but fortunately there are still some musicians who dare to think outside the box, giving rise to such marvels as this Telecaster. Note the single sound hole typical of the Thinline design, but with a rather flashy Champagne sparkle finish. The Filter'Tron neck pickup, small-format scratchplate (it has been taken off, but the holes for it can still be seen) and Sperzel machine heads hark back to the Cabronita model (its name a diminutive of a mild Spanish swearword), a Custom Shop take on the notion of a Tele with a Filter'Tron (i.e. a Fender/Gretsch hybrid) that started off as a limited edition and ended up inspiring a range of Squier guitars. Note also the reversed control plate (with the pickup selector at the back and the knobs at the front) and the RSD bridge, which combines the traditional sound of the three bridge saddles of the vintage design with compensation for intonation, proof that you can still improve details on a 75-year-old model.

Years of manufacture: 2010s
Country: United States
Approximate resale value: £4,200
Hear it on: Tom Jones, 'Talking Reality Television Blues' (2021)
Guitarist: Scott McKeon

# Fender Jaguar

**The Jaguar was the last classic model to be designed by Leo Fender for the brand that bears his name, and it was also a dismal failure, even though it was created specifically to address the expectations of contemporary guitarists. That was not the end of the story, however, and the Jaguar was to have its revenge.**

•

When Fender brought out the Jazzmaster, the company was hoping – as the name of the model might suggest – to appeal to the jazz musicians who until then had made up a large portion of Gibson's clientèle. The jazzers failed to respond, however, and it was eventually surf guitarists who fell for the charms of the diminutive new arrival's colourful offset look.

Fender sought to capitalize on this success in 1962 by releasing a new model aimed specifically at surf musicians. The Jaguar took its name from the world of motoring (rather than being an animal reference) and echoed the Jazzmaster's quirky body shape, although with some differences in the dimensions. At first sight, the Jaguar's appearance is dominated by the enormous quantity of chrome, with three control plates, the vibrato, the bridge and even the pickup surrounds. Most significantly, however, it was the brand's first model to be fitted with a 22-fret fingerboard (rather than 21) and a short-scale, 61cm (24in) neck more diminutive even than Gibson's (63cm/24¾in) and far reduced from Fender's usual long-scale length (64.8cm/25½in), giving a more elastic feel when playing with less resistance. It also featured a mute – a strip of foam that could be raised against the strings at the bridge to achieve the plunky surf sound without having to palm-mute with the right hand.

The Jaguar was expensive, however, being the brand's top-of-the-range guitar, and it failed to find an audience. After a long absence from the catalogue, it was eventually rediscovered by the indie rock musicians of the 1990s, with Kurt Cobain leading the charge, and has become one of Fender's essential models. Collectors go mad for vintage examples, especially when they are as sought-after as this mint-condition 1964 in the extremely rare custom colour of Shell Pink, with gold hardware.

Year of manufacture: 1964
Country: United States
Approximate resale value: in this colour, £25,000;
in standard sunburst, £8,300
Hear it on: Red Hot Chili Peppers,
'Around the World' (1999)
Guitarist: John Frusciante

Fender
JAGUAR
INSTRUCTION MANUAL
Covered in Luxurious
TOLEX
as advertised in....
HOLIDAY
NORMAL
VOLUME
TREBLE
BASS
INTENSITY
Vibroverb Amp
FENDER ELECT. INST. CO.
DESIGN & CIRCUITS PATENTED
Fender

**Fender Jaguar**

The Jaguar vibrato was the same as the Jazzmaster's, a system designed as an improvement on the Stratocaster's synchronized tremolo but which failed to achieve the same success. Gold hardware is extremely rare on a Fender, unlike with Gretsch (on the White Falcon) or Gibson (the Les Paul Custom), for example.

NORMAL
BRIGHT
1
2
VOLUME
Fender
VIBROLUX ®
REVERB

# Fender
## B-Bender Telecaster

**The B-Bender is an entirely mechanical lever system that takes the principle of a pedal steel guitar and applies it to a Telecaster. This inspired invention and its very distinctive sound date to 1967, and it has since inspired guitarists from a wide variety of styles.**

•

We have the guitarist Clarence White and drummer Gene Parsons (who also played banjo, harmonica and guitar) to thank for the B-Bender, which dates from the time when both were members of the group Nashville West, before they joined the Byrds. The idea had been inspired by the pedal steel guitar, an instrument derived from the lap steel, which was played in a sitting position with the neck face up, using foot-operated pedals and levers pushed with the knees to alter the pitch of one or more strings. As the name suggests, the B-Bender concentrated its efforts on the B string (the second-thinnest string), which the player could raise a whole tone to C# by applying pressure to the guitar strap.

White showcased the possibilities of the system with a talent bordering on genius during the Byrds' live performances in 1969, as well as for session work with the Everly Brothers, Joe Cocker and Arlo Guthrie. His career came to a tragic end when he was killed by a drunk driver in 1973, whereupon the singer Marty Stuart took ownership of the famous 1954 Telecaster in which White had installed the prototype B-Bender (the guitar shown here), and which he still owns to this day.

Parsons had long been installing B-Benders himself at the request of musicians, and other systems have also been created as variations on the principle. This very distinctive sound can be heard from Jimmy Page ('All My Love'), Mike Campbell (throughout Mudcrutch's first, eponymous album), Albert Lee, Brent Mason and Brad Paisley (who used a G-Bender rather than a B), and it is highly likely that the system will continue to inspire curious guitarists.

Year of manufacture: 1954
Country: United States
Approximate resale value:
if this historic instrument were ever put up for auction, maybe £584,000;
for a close approximation made by the Custom Shop, £6,700
Hear it on: The Byrds, 'Drug Store Truck Drivin' Man' (*Live at the Fillmore*, 1969)
Guitar solo: Clarence White

NUDIE
Fender
FENDER
PAT. PEND

Taylor as luthier and Listug handling administration and marketing. Between them, they had cooked up a vision that was radically different from what had gone before; the big brands were resting on their laurels with frankly average production values, their freedom to experiment hampered by the large corporations of which they were a part.

Taylor's independence and determination to make a difference brought about a number of revolutions in the acoustic world. The firm standardized necks that were as thin and comfortable as electrics (at a time when acoustic necks tended to be baseball bats), and designed several reliable electro-acoustic systems to provide a proper sound for guitarists appearing on stage.

In half a century of existence, the Californian brand has progressed from a small workshop to two factories (in the USA and Mexico) employing 750 staff, and the quest for new ways of improving the instruments has never ceased. The Builder's Edition series are Taylor's top-of-the-range models, and this superb 912ce features many characteristics typical of the brand's personality. Even the model number will tell you a lot if you know how to read it: the '9' represents its position in the range (which is numbered from 1 to 9, from simplest to most luxurious) and the '12' is for the compact Grand Concert shape; 'c 'stands for cutaway and 'e' for electro-acoustic.

In addition to having the perfect dimensions for musicians in search of ultimate comfort, the BE 912ce also boasts an armrest (a chamfer for the right forearm) and even another gentle chamfer scooped out of the cutaway. Such features had previously been the preserve of exclusive, luthier-made instruments, but Taylor has made them more accessible.

Year of manufacture: 2020
Country: United States
Approximate resale value: £3,300
Hear it on: Dave Matthews Band, 'Walk Around the Moon' (2023)
Guitarist: Dave Matthews

# Gibson
## Trini Lopez

**Because of his poppier side, Trini Lopez is the exception among the perfectly creditable band of jazz guitarists who have won the right to a signature model from Gibson. That distinction can be seen in this guitar, which is infinitely more similar to the brand's ES-335 than it is to an archtop.**

•

When Les Paul chose not to renew his contract with Gibson in 1962, it became more important than ever to continue to shore up the Kalamazoo manufacturer's reputation for excellence with models bearing the name of high-profile artists. The Gibson management was not particularly drawn to rock 'n' roll, so they settled on jazz artists, such as Johnny Smith, Tal Farlow, Barney Kessel and, for the Epiphone line, Al Caiola and Howard Roberts.

Trinidad 'Trini' Lopez, a 27-year-old pop-folk singer of Mexican heritage who had been discovered by Frank Sinatra, found himself in the middle of all this activity. He had scored a notable success with his version of 'If I Had a Hammer' in 1963 (yes, the song recorded by Peter, Paul and Mary a year earlier), and in 1964 he attached his name to not one but two signature Gibson models: the Deluxe (or Custom), which adopted more or less the same architecture as the Barney Kessel Regular model he had been using previously (a large archtop with two pointed horns); and the Standard, which featured two rounded horns and the quarter-body structure with a central block used for the ES-335. Both models had the same diamond-shaped sound holes, a special feature that distinguished them immediately from the rest of the series, plus a headstock with six in-line machine heads, a layout that was reused for the non-reverse Firebird on the Standard and, with a slightly quirkier shape, on the Custom.

Apart from these cosmetic differences, the Standard is essentially an ES-335 in all its glory, with the minor distinction that the tailpiece is farther from the bridge. Dave Grohl has made it his guitar of choice, and the superb example shown here, in very rare Pelham Blue, is owned by the producer John Shanks (Bon Jovi).

Year of manufacture: 1966 or 1967
Country: United States
Approximate resale value: for this historic instrument in this custom colour, £16,700; in a standard red finish, £6,700
Hear it on: Foo Fighters, 'This Is a Call' (1995)
Guitarist: Dave Grohl

TRINI
LOPEZ

**that symbolizes a particular approach to the guitar that is as unsophisticated as possible. On the other, it is proof that any instrument can be an underground success; all you need is a good musician to unlock the potential the rest of the world has overlooked.**

•

The Les Paul model sold pretty well in 1954. Gibson's first solid-body was only available in a Gold Top finish at the time, and the brand wished to capitalize on its success by offering variants on the theme, much as a car manufacturer might create a range from a single model. This historic manufacturer designed the Les Paul Custom, a more luxurious version, with a view to establishing it for good as a respected model within its catalogue, rather than just a passing fad.

However, Gibson also wanted to appeal to guitarists who were less well-off, and to offer lucky beginners an instrument worthy of the firm's name and cheaper than Fender's Esquire of the time. The starting point was the price, a very psychological US$99, and they worked backwards from there to design an instrument that could be sold for that amount, which meant no more maple caps and a simple mahogany body with no carving. There were no luxury inlays or fret markers, just dots for the fretboard and a logo, but also – most importantly – there was just one pickup, a single P90 at the bridge. It stayed a P90 even when the other models in the range evolved towards a humbucker in 1957, in much the same way that the bridge remained a wraparound after the rest of the range had progressed to a Tune-O-Matic in 1955. Simple.

The guitar was basic but highly effective, and it was Leslie West of the band Mountain who was the first to fully appreciate the sonic virtues of this modest P90 on its slab of mahogany. From that moment onwards, the Junior was a rock and punk staple, a symbol of a direct approach to sound and songs for such heroes as Keith Richards, Johnny Thunders (the New York Dolls) and Billie Joe Armstrong (Green Day).

Year of manufacture: 1958
Country: United States
Approximate resale value: £10,000
Hear it on: Mountain, 'Mississippi Queen' (1970)
Guitarist: Leslie West

# Martin
## D-28

**Collectors and fans of great vintage guitars automatically tend to describe as the Holy Grail any instrument that is highly sought-after and extremely rare, such as the Burst among electrics. For acoustics, however, there is nothing more desirable than a pre-war D-28.**

•

That is the dream for acoustic collectors, but it is also for the vast majority of guitarists a sonic benchmark, the yardstick against which all modern dreadnoughts are to be judged. Martins from the 1930s have been dubbed 'pre-war' or 'golden-era', and true connoisseurs will get the reference before the brand is even mentioned. The finest country, folk and rock musicians, from Hank Williams and Jerry Garcia to Neil Young and Bob Dylan, recorded their greatest albums on pre-war D-28s.

The D-28 is the 'standard' rosewood dreadnought model, with a soundboard of Adirondack spruce and a body of Brazilian rosewood. The use of these two woods in the pre-war D-28 plays a major part in the fascination the model exerts upon musicians; many have rather hastily decided that these are the best possible woods without really having tried anything else, since the legendary status of Martins from this era is impossible to gainsay. This appeal has only been reinforced by the ban on sawn rosewood from Rio, which has made it unobtainable and therefore even more desirable.

Visually, pre-war D-28s can be identified by the herringbone binding around the soundboard, which was present from 1934 until about 1946, during which period fewer than a thousand or so guitars were manufactured. For that reason, herringbone D-28s (often just called 'herringbones') are rare and very expensive. Reissues and high-end copies abound, but holding an original in your hands is always a deeply moving experience.

Year of manufacture: 1938
Country: United States
Approximate resale value: £58,400
Hear it on: Neil Young, 'This Old Guitar' (2005)

# Fender
## 1959 Jazzmaster

**From the release of his first solid-body electric model, in 1950, Leo Fender never ceased to reimagine his designs with a view to inventing the ultimate guitar, which would of course be placed at the very top of the catalogue. The Jazzmaster was supposed to be that high point, but it turned out to be the Californian brand's first dud.**

•

Fender had had a big hit with the Stratocaster in 1954, just four years after designing the Broadcaster, its first model (which became the Telecaster). Leo Fender was not the type to rest on his laurels, however, and four years later, in 1958, he brought out his third solid-body electric guitar, intending it to supplant the Strat as the most luxurious in the manufacturer's range. The new arrival was to cost US$329, compared to the Strat's US$275.

There were several differences to explain this jump in pricing. The Jazzmaster was the first Fender to feature a rosewood fretboard, which was viewed as an improvement borrowed from Gibson's refined styling. It also had pickups with a rounder, warmer sound than the Stratocaster, controlled by two separate systems, as well as a new, specially designed vibrato with a smoother action than the synchronized tremolo fitted to the Strat. The first models were also equipped with the famous gold-coloured anodized-aluminium scratchplate that can be seen on this guitar, whose blond finish (white with visible grain) over an ash body (rather than the standard alder) makes it particularly rare and desirable.

Despite these so-called improvements, the Jazzmaster's radical appearance (with its offset waist) and complex controls prevented it from finding favour with the public. To this day, it remains less popular than the two Fender models that preceded it.

Year of manufacture: 1959
Country: United States
Approximate resale value:
in this extremely rare white finish, £29,200;
in sunburst with a tortoiseshell scratchplate,
£12,500
Hear it on: Television, 'Marquee Moon' (1977)
Guitarist: Tom Verlaine

VOLUME
TONE

# LES PAUL

## THE MAN BEHIND THE GUITAR

**The Gibson Les Paul has become such an essential point of reference that its origin has almost been forgotten. Many musicians play a Les Paul every day but have no idea about the man behind their instrument.**

•

Gibson has even gone as far as creating signature Les Pauls for such artists as Jimmy Page, Joe Perry, Buckethead and many others, effectively making them double signature models. The most important name is still the first, however, and Les Paul casts a long shadow over the popular music of the 20th century for several reasons.

Lester William Polsfuss was born in 1915 in Wisconsin to middle-class parents of German descent. He took a very early interest in singing, dancing, music and DIY, and by the age of seven he had modified his mother's player piano to change the tunes it played. He began to learn the harmonica at eight, then moved on to the guitar, quickly turning professional under the pseudonyms Red Hot Red and Rhubarb Red before finally becoming Les Paul.

Paul was among the first to try out experimental solid-body electric guitars, starting with a length of railway track fitted with a telephone receiver wired to a radio. The results sounded good but the audience were not prepared for the device's futuristic lines, so he added wings to make it look like a traditional archtop, learning the important lesson that, in the public mind, an instrument sounded good only if it looked good.

This spirit of invention was not limited to the guitar, however, and Paul was one of the first musicians to install a professional-level studio in his garage. It was there that he invented overdubbing, a method of recording several superimposed takes of the same instrument – so every musical artist is in his debt to some extent.

Paul applied these methods to the tracks he recorded with the singer Mary Ford at the end of the 1940s, and the duo scored several big hits that brought them a regular television show on NBC. Gibson sought to capitalize on this exposure by offering Paul a signature model of its first solid-body guitar, with results that must have been beyond its wildest dreams.

# Fender
## Custom Shop Relic Stratocaster

**With the prices of vintage guitars rising to the point of becoming entirely beyond the reach of most musicians, brands are coming up with ever more plausible replicas of their past glories. As has often been the case, the brand from California has led the charge.**

•

The idea of manufacturing a new object that looks old is hardly revolutionary, and even in the world of guitars there had been pioneers before the phenomenon skyrocketed at Fender. Repairers might age certain components to match old instruments under restoration, and some luthiers created fake vintage guitars to which they gave an apparent patina. The real spark came at the end of the 1980s, however, and in 1987 Fender created the Custom Shop, a small team of elite luthiers charged with making bespoke instruments for star customers. John Page, the head of the Custom Shop, took on the luthier J W Black in 1989, and Black later met Vince Cunetto, a painter of genius who could reproduce the wear and tear on an old Fender.

Together, they cooked up replicas of Stratocasters and Telecasters from the 1950s and presented them at the 1995 NAMM Show without telling a soul. Even the experts were fooled, and such replicas have since been available from the Custom Shop as 'relics' – an almost perfect name, given the semi-religious fascination exerted by vintage guitars. Demand for these instruments has grown exponentially, to such a point that the Fender Custom Shop now offers several levels of ageing and makes scarcely any guitars that look new. Other brands, such as Gibson, Gretsch and even Martin, have followed suit and now also offer 'fake vintage' guitars.

This relic belonging to the blues musician Tyler Bryant has all the characteristics of a shell-pink Stratocaster from 1960. This is part of the magic of a relic; you can easily find an instrument that looks vintage, with specifications perfectly suited to your playing style.

Year of manufacture: 2000s
Country: United States
Approximate resale value: £2,900
Hear it on: Tyler Bryant & the Shakedown, 'The Wayside' (2015)

VOLUME
TONE

# Airline
# J B Hutto

**Not every American guitar from the 1960s was a Strat or an SG. Countless guitars made in the second half of the decade came from the factories of cheap instrument manufacturers based in Chicago, as was the case with this beautiful oddity, which eventually rose to recognition in the 2000s.**

•

Valco was Kay's big competitor, and the two conglomerates supplied several brands with instruments that, while undoubtedly manufactured in the United States (in Chicago, in these two cases), fell far short in the assembly quality and wood selection of the standards required in Fullerton or Kalamazoo. This was a deliberate choice intended to provide cheap guitars for those beginners who had picked up the instrument after the arrival of the Beatles on that side of the Atlantic in 1964.

Valco was named after its three founders, Victor Smith, Al Frost and Louis Dopyera (one of Dobro's Dopyera brothers), and manufactured instruments branded Supro, National, Oahu and Airline. In particular, they made guitars out of fibreglass (renamed Res-O-Glas), including this signature model for the Chicago bluesman J B Hutto, with two pickups that are in fact single coils despite their humbucking appearance.

By the end of the 1960s Japanese guitar manufacturing had begun to make a name for itself among American beginners with even keener pricing for far better quality. As a result, sales plummeted for the Chicago behemoths, to the extent that Valco bought up Kay in 1967 before shutting up shop the following year.

The guitars produced by the two groups were among the instruments that could be bought for a song in American pawnshops during the 1980s and 90s, until Jack White made a J B Hutto his main instrument for the best part of a decade with the White Stripes. Airlines suddenly became desirable, other groups picked up on them, and they are now sought-after vintage guitars that have been copied and reissued by other brands.

Year of manufacture: 1965
Country: United States
Approximate resale value: £2,100
Hear it on: The White Stripes, 'Black Math' (2003)
Guitarist: Jack White

# Fender
## Antigua Coronado II

**Fender fans are in general agreement that CBS's acquisition of the brand in 1965 marked the end of the golden age and the beginning of a period in which the quality of the instruments dropped off considerably. Despite all this, there were new designs with much to recommend them, such as this superb Coronado.**

•

The Beatles touched down in the United States in 1964 and the electric guitar market exploded in their wake. There were some who sensed a profit to be made, including the CBS (Columbia Broadcasting System) media group, which bought Fender for a colossal sum in 1965. Leo Fender became an independent consultant to the company, but his original designs (the Tele, the Strat, the Jazzmaster and the Jaguar, plus all the basses) were never subsequently matched.

Having previously designed key models for Rickenbacker, Roger Rossmeisl, a luthier from Germany with a keen eye for aesthetics, was employed by Fender at this time, and when the company asked him to work on a quarter-body guitar, he came up with the Coronado. The idea was to compete with the Epiphone Casino (which had benefited greatly from the so-called Beatles effect), as well as to extend the palette of sounds available from the Fender catalogue beyond solid-body guitars.

Despite its quarter-body design (which is fully hollow, with no centre block) and the two rounded horns inspired by the ES-330, the Coronado retained certain visual and technical calling cards of a Fender, such as its bolt-on neck and a headstock with six-in-line machine heads reminiscent of the Stratocaster.

The most distinctive characteristic of this model resulted from an accident, however. Fender employees were not used to applying binding to a quarter-body guitar, and some examples turned up with burn marks that had blackened the edges of the top. To hide these faults, Fender invented the gradated Antigua finish that went from black to a greyish mustard-yellow in the centre. This finish was subsequently made available as an option for all the models in Fender's range, and it became a typical choice in the 1970s, but it was never as perfect as on the Coronado II.

Year of manufacture: 1967
Country: United States
Approximate resale value: £3,300
Hear it on: The Flaming Lips, 'Turn It On' (1993)
Guitarist: Wayne Coyne

CORONADO II
EFFECTS
REMOTE
ECHO
CANCEL REMOTE SW.

# Gibson
## Hummingbird

**As the 1960s got underway, Gibson began to give its guitars increasingly eccentric looks. The company's acoustics had until then been spared the outlandish designs used for the electrics (such as the Explorer and the Flying V), leaving musicians a choice between the ornate, outsize J-200, whose design dated back to the 1930s, and the wholly sober lines of the J-45.**

•

It is difficult to believe, given the brand's somewhat austere reputation, but the inspiration for Gibson's more fun acoustic guitars came from Martin, starting with the first guitar to take on the original dreadnought shape. Up to this point, Gibsons had had a slope shoulder design, but the advent in 1960 of the Hummingbird with its square shoulders brought Nazareth shapes to Kalamazoo.

It had all the typical ingredients of a Gibson, of course, with the same essential elements as a J-45 (spruce top, mahogany body and neck, rosewood fretboard and bridge), but the decoration was much more similar to a J-200, with a scratchplate covered in patterns of flowers that were clearly being enjoyed by the eponymous hummingbird.

Thanks to its classic Gibson look and sound, the Hummingbird was a massive success, to the point that the brand could hardly keep up with orders. Meanwhile, in 1962 Gibson launched the Dove, its second square-shoulder model, which picked up on the avian theme but used the same wood as the J-200, having a maple body and neck.

The Dove did not prove as popular as the Hummingbird, so Gibson hit upon a genius idea. In 1963 the company took all the unsold Doves, put a hummingbird scratchplate on them and sold them as Hummingbirds, showing how much less picky brands and musicians were about the objective characteristics of guitars than they are today. This hybrid model, which was produced only in 1963 and is shown here, is known by collectors as the Hummingdove.

Year of manufacture: 1963
Country: United States
Approximate resale value: £8,300
Hear it on: The Rolling Stones, 'Street Fighting Man' (1968)
Guitarist: Keith Richards

# Gibson
# 1958 Les Paul Standard

**No electric guitar is more desirable than a Burst, and none has so clearly defined the sound of blues, rock and hard rock. The Les Paul Standard from the late 1950s has inspired more fantasies, urban legends and absurd speculation, and attracted more attempted copies and (mostly) faithful reissues, than any other.**

•

In 1957 the Les Paul Gold Top was fitted with the humbucking pickups that Gibson had just created, but this beautiful gold guitar still struggled to find an appreciative audience. Indeed, its appearance did seem rather dated compared to the Fenders that evoked the sounds and scents of a Californian beach. In addition, Paul's moment of glory had passed and for many people the model was no longer particularly exciting. In mid-1958 Gibson decided to change the finish to make it more attractive. It was renamed the Les Paul Standard (which located it between the Special and the Custom) and given a maple cap in cherry sunburst, a finish that ran from red to a light orange for the best effect. The public still failed to bite, however, and the model was discontinued at the end of 1960; by then, 1,712 Les Paul sunbursts had been manufactured over fewer than three years.

In 1965 Eric Clapton, an ambitious young British musician, bought one of these guitars second-hand and used it to record a legendary album with John Mayall & the Bluesbreakers. In 1966, across the Pond, it was the American Mike Bloomfield who was making his Burst ring out like no other. From that moment, every guitarist was after the same sound and wanted to get their hands on this extremely rare model – and that's without even mentioning the vintage guitar market.

These days, Bursts are still cult items that change hands among collectors for ludicrous sums, and the few musicians with access to a period example only reinforce its mystique. This particular 1958 belongs to Greg Martin, guitarist of the Kentucky Headhunters, and was given to him by the country singer Hank Williams Jr in 1993.

Year of manufacture: 1958
Country: United States
Approximate resale value: £166,800
Hear it on: The Rolling Stones, 'Midnight Rambler'
(live – *Get Yer Ya-Ya's Out!*, 1970)
Guitarist: Mick Taylor

# PRS
## Custom 24

**By the 1980s the historic brands were flagging, and it was at this time that different designs began to emerge and find favour with the most demanding musicians. Of these new designs, Paul Reed Smith's guitars fared so well that they have now become the third giant in the electric guitar world.**

•

Gibson and Fender production in the 1980s was not up to the standards of the instruments that had established the reputations of these historic brands, and that led to a desire for alternative visions from other manufacturers. The Superstrat (a Stratocaster with Gibson-style pickups) was omnipresent, but the luthier Paul Reed Smith had other ideas.

In his workshop in Maryland, he took the two-horned shape of the late 1950s Les Paul Junior and gave it the carved maple cap of a Les Paul Standard (generally using highly flamed maple), a 24-fret neck in the style of the shredder guitars of the time, and a vibrato system that had been inspired by the Strat but was more efficient. The result was the PRS Custom 24 (for the number of frets), a model he unveiled in 1985 and which immediately won the hearts of musicians of the stature of Carlos Santana and Howard Leese (Heart).

PRS has become a veritable empire, a brand that sells guitars made in the United States as well as an Indonesian range, amplifiers and even effects pedals. The Custom 24 has become one of the classic models of guitar history and a standard feature of many styles, from blues to metal.

Year of manufacture: 2000s
Country: United States
Approximate resale value: £2,500
Hear it on: Porcupine Tree, 'Blackest Eyes' (2002)
Guitarist: Steven Wilson

**PRS Custom 24**

Paul Reed Smith is constantly striving to improve every detail of his instruments with a view to achieving a perfect guitar shape that does not buck tradition. You can see the scooped cutaway of this Custom 24 that allows better access to the highest notes. The cutaway also shows the maple cap on top of the mahogany body.

# Fender
## CBS Stratocaster

**The electric guitar market became so lucrative in the mid-1960s that it began to attract the interest of enormous conglomerates. The era's biggest takeover was CBS's purchase of Fender in 1965. This change soon had clear repercussions for the instruments themselves, such as this Stratocaster, which is a typical example for the period.**

•

The Beatles' appearance on the *Ed Sullivan Show* on 9 February 1964 sparked a profound cultural revolution, and overnight every young American wanted an electric guitar. The big brands – which had until then been modestly proportioned companies – suddenly found it hard to keep up with demand, even though they were making money hand over fist (Fender in particular). Leo Fender was having health problems that prevented him from devoting himself to his business, so he decided to sell. Negotiations with the Baldwin piano brand came to nothing (that firm later took its revenge by purchasing Gretsch in 1967), and CBS eventually took ownership of Fender on 5 January 1965 for the astronomical sum of US$13 million (about $130 million today).

CBS was an enormous group that also owned the CBS television channel (which broadcast the very same *Ed Sullivan Show*), the New York Yankees baseball team and some 40 other companies. After taking over Fender, it tried to make the brand even more profitable, resulting in a drop in instrument quality – and that is why 'pre-CBS' guitars have become particularly sought-after.

This decline was, of course, gradual, and there were still very good Strats to be found until the end of the 1960s (Jimi Hendrix didn't seem too upset with his new instruments from the period). The most obvious cosmetic change dates from 1966, with the famous big headstock, the point of which was to make the logo more visible. This polarized Strat fans: some found it a deal-breaker while others actively sought it out. A 'transition' logo is clearly visible on some guitars, an intermediate stage between the smaller spaghetti logo and the black logo from 1968 that truly defines this change of era.

Year of manufacture: 1966
Country: United States
Approximate resale value: £10,000
Hear it on: Jimi Hendrix, 'Machine Gun' (1970)

INSTRUMENTS
VIBRO CHAMP
BASS
SPEED
INTENSITY
OFF
Fender
NORMAL
VOLUME
TREBLE
BASS
VOLUME
REVERB
SPEED
INTENSITY
Deluxe Reverb-Amp
FENDER MUSICAL INSTRUMENTS
Fender
VOLUME
TONE
TONE

# Music Man
## St Vincent Goldie

**The story of the electric guitar is by no means a thing of the past. It continues to progress thanks to musicians who invent new ways of using the instrument, and to brands that respond to that vision. St Vincent is a major figure among such musicians, with an extraordinary personality to match, and the Music Man model that bears her name has been created in her image.**

•

America's St Vincent (real name Annie Clark) is not only an excellent guitarist but also a singer, songwriter and fully rounded artist with an established back catalogue and a host of awards to her name. In common with many guitarists, she is also a gearhead, always on the lookout for very particular sounds to expand her range. That is why she released her first signature model with Ernie Ball/Music Man in 2016. Music Man was the second brand launched by Leo Fender after Fender was bought up by CBS, initially in secret with two former Fender employees (with an obligatory confidentiality clause), then openly in 1974. Music Man was purchased by the Ernie Ball string brand ten years later, since which time the Ernie Ball/Music Man catalogue has been based on signature models for such major artists as John Petrucci, Albert Lee, Steve Morse and Steve Lukather.

The first St Vincent model featured three mini humbuckers for a unique configuration nicely showcased in a body shape that was both retro and cutting-edge. On releasing the overtly 1970s-sounding album *Daddy's Home* in 2021, St Vincent designed the Goldie, her second model, which took its nickname from its gold foil pickups, inspired by Japanese guitars from the 1960s and 70s. The result – illustrated here in a luscious velveteen finish – is modern, timeless and fascinating, all at the same time.

Year of manufacture: 2021
Country: United States
Approximate resale value: £1,700
Hear it on: St Vincent, 'Live in the Dream' (2021)

MUSICMAN

# Rickenbacker 366/12

**Much like Gretsch, Rickenbacker belongs to the exclusive, fairly diminutive club of brands that form an essential part of any collection, and for the same reason. These are guitars with their own unique sound. If you have room for only one Rickenbacker in your collection, it must be a 12-string.**

•

Rickenbacker did not invent the 12-string electric, but it is a fair bet that this would never have become an icon of the sound of the 1960s if the brand had not made the design its own. Before the prototype 360/12 of 1963, which sparked the whole revolution, there had been only the 12-string neck on Gibson's double-neck and Danelectro's exotic Bellzouki. That said, there had been any number of 12-string acoustics, and this is probably where Rickenbacker's inspiration is to be found, not least since the fashion for folk music was in full swing at the time.

The Beatles made their first foray across to the United States at the turn of 1964, and Francis Hall, president of Rickenbacker, met the band in their New York hotel to show them the prototype. George Harrison was immediately struck by the design's potential, and the 360/12 was to play a central role in the song 'A Hard Day's Night' a few months later. In the United States, the singer and guitarist Roger McGuinn heard its jangly sound and made it his trademark with his group, the Byrds. From this point onwards, the sound of the electric 12-string was an essential element of the hippy era, and Rickenbacker has now become indelibly associated with the movement.

This 366/12 model was produced from 1965 until 1975 and is typical of the ideas of the time: interesting, but of doubtful practical use, a fact that may explain why it did not last. The metal comb mutes the octave strings by pulling them downwards, transforming the 12-string (with its staggered machine heads) into a 6-string. That was the theory, at least, but in practice, these instruments are mostly very beautiful vintage 12-strings with many a story to tell.

Year of manufacture: 1966
Country: United States
Approximate resale value: £4,200
Hear it on: The Byrds, 'Mr. Tambourine Man' (1965)
Guitarist: Roger McGuinn

BRIGHT
VOLUME
REVERB
SPEED
Reverb-Amp
ELECTRIC INSTRUMENT CO.
DESIGN & CIRCUITS
PATENTED 62

# Fender Jazzmaster Custom Colour

**The 1960s was a decade of colour at Fender, and no model lent itself quite so well to the custom colour palette as the Jazzmaster. Despite the model's contemporary lack of success, it summed up its era perfectly and enjoyed a veritable resurrection in the 1980s.**

•

The combination of Fender guitars' simplicity of construction and their designs, which were typical of the culture of fun in Space Age California, made the instruments perfect vehicles for extravagant colour schemes. Whereas Gibson had half a century of history weighing on its shoulders and some well-established habits, Fender was still enjoying all the insouciance of youth and could allow itself a few indiscretions.

For Fender, any colour that was not standard was by definition a custom colour: in other words, every Telecaster that was not blond and every Stratocaster or Jazzmaster that was not sunburst. Technically, even a blond Stratocaster was a custom colour. The official catalogue of available colours released in 1960, less than two years after the launch of the Jazzmaster, contained fifteen hues borrowed from the car industry. The Jazzmaster's offset design made it an ideal canvas for Fiesta Red or Lake Placid Blue (as seen here), especially with the option of having a matching headstock.

As the name might suggest, the Jazzmaster was intended to appeal to so-called proper guitarists, the jazzers who played a lot more Gibsons, but none of these fell very much in love with the diminutive new arrival. It was briefly the darling of surf musicians before slipping into oblivion. Eventually, however, the post-punk and indie rock guitarists of the 1980s and 90s turned it into an iconic model whose sonic qualities are still being explored and revealed.

Year of manufacture: 1962
Country: United States
Approximate resale value: £16,700
Hear it on: Dinosaur Jr, 'Start Choppin'' (1993)
Guitarist: J Mascis

Fender
FINE ELECTRIC INSTRUMENTS
VOLUME
TONE

# Gibson ES-5 Switchmaster

**Guitarists have always been receptive to the notion of several uses for their instrument, and are not averse to the idea of a lavishly ornate guitar. There was a time when the Switchmaster represented the epitome of both these points of view.**

•

Before the ES-5 there had been the L-5, created by the luthier and inventor Lloyd Loar in 1922. That was the first guitar to have a curved soundboard and F-holes – in other words the model that ushered in the archtop jazz guitar as we know it today. As the company's catalogue developed, the L-5 stayed up to date by adopting a series of new features, including a larger body and a cutaway. Gibson eventually made it the company's top-of-the-range electric model in 1949, rechristening it the ES-5.

The ES-5 was highly ornate, with several layers of binding (including around the headstock), striking fretboard markers, blingy gold hardware and a flamed maple soundboard magnificently set off by its natural finish. It was also the first electric guitar in history to feature three pickups, five years before the Stratocaster that was to become the industry standard. At the time, Gibson had not known exactly how to help guitarists get the best sound out of these three P90s, and had simply installed a volume control for each, allowing the musician to blend the three sounds as if on a mixing board.

In 1955, however, the ES-5 became the ES-5 Switchmaster, thanks to a four-way switch that allowed the user to select each pickup individually or have all three on at once. The bridge became even more ostentatious the following year with the advent of the double-loop model, and in 1957 the P90s were eventually replaced with Gibson's new humbucking pickups.

The Switchmaster has been in the vanguard of Gibson's look and sound throughout its existence, appealing to guitarists as varied as T-Bone Walker, Frank Zappa, Carl Perkins and Steve Howe.

Year of manufacture: 1957
Country: United States
Approximate resale value: £12,500
Hear it on: The Mothers of Invention, 'Trouble Every Day' (1968)
Guitarist: Frank Zappa

1 2 3 ALL

beginner with their first guitar and any number of local musicians with the last instrument they will ever need.

Some of their guitars have made their way to places closer at hand, however, in particular the United Kingdom because of the privileged links between Commonwealth countries. In June 1963, when the Beatles were about to explode on to the general scene, George Harrison took his Gretsch for repair to a Manchester guitar shop that lent him this Maton MS500 (MS for Mastersound) as a replacement. There are photos of the Beatle with this very guitar in his hands, in particular from the last gig the group ever played at the Cavern Club in Liverpool (the small venue where they learned their trade), having played a total of 292 concerts there since 1961. It's quite the symbol.

This museum piece has sold several times at auction, but it is not the only Maton to have found favour outside its native Australia. The charismatic Josh Homme, lead singer of the Queens of the Stone Age, has his signature model (a semi-hollow electric) with the brand. However, it is the acoustic stars Tommy Emmanuel (Australia) and John Butler (California) in particular who have spread the name of Maton throughout the world, to the point that their electro-acoustic guitars are now the most sought-after and renowned models in the catalogue.

Year of manufacture: 1963
Country: Australia
Approximate resale value: this example, which belonged to George Harrison, £667,300 at auction; without such provenance, £2,500
Hear it on: Queens of the Stone Age, 'Turnin' on the Screw' (2007)
Guitarist: Josh Homme

Maton
VOX
M.S.500
Bigsby

**Maton MS500**

Depending on the way a guitar is stored, the variations in temperature and humidity it endures and the composition of the original lacquer, the finish can age very differently. With this very beautiful headstock, the brand logo and design have survived, but the lacquer and paint have cracked to the point of flaking off at the edges.

# Martin
## 00-45S

**Martin is without doubt the most important brand in the history of the modern guitar and an American institution to which we are indebted for many innovations that we now take for granted. That is why it is always moving to come face-to-face with an instrument as old and pioneering as this 00-45S.**

•

The origins of Martin take us to the Old World and the town of Markneukirchen in Saxony, Germany. Christian Friedrich Martin was born into a family of cabinetmakers in 1796 and learned his craft as a luthier apprenticed to Stauffer in Vienna. On returning to Germany, he found that the guild system prevented him from practising his trade as he would have liked, so he moved to New York in 1833 before settling in 1838 in Nazareth, Pennsylvania, the small town where the Martin factory has been ever since.

In the meantime, Martin had been working on improving the design of his guitars, introducing innovative X-bracing that was to revolutionize the instrument. This bracing system, which reinforces the soundboard, made it possible to use steel (rather than gut) strings to produce a radically different sound that would eventually become standard and, in the distant future, even allow the instrument to be electrified.

The Martin range breaks down into several shapes classified by size, and the standard designations were 0 and 00, from the very smallest to the largest (which arrived in the 1910s). The second set of digits in the model number indicates the woods used and the level of ornamentation, from 15 (all mahogany, no ornamentation) to 45 (spruce top, rosewood body, maximum decoration). This sublime 00 from 1902 is in fact a prototype 45 (a model that would not appear officially for another two years), making this 00-42S incredibly rare. Besides the inlaid binding on front and back, around the sound hole, along the fretboard and on the bridge pins, note the highly ornate, mandolin-style scratchplate, ivory bridge and tree-of-life inlay running the length of the fretboard. This guitar is a work of art, a historical object and a musical instrument, all at the same time.

Year of manufacture: 1902
Country: United States
Approximate resale value: £166,800
Hear it on: John Mayer, 'Queen of California' (2012)

# Fender
## Electric XII

**The electric 12-string was at the height of fashion in the mid-1960s, an icon that symbolizes the moment when folk music set about transforming itself into Flower Power psychedelia as it moved from the coffee shops of New York to the beaches of the West Coast. Fender clearly had to be involved.**

•

The 12-string acoustic is one of the most important instruments in folk music, being a good way of providing backing for a singer with no other accompaniment than their own guitar. However, the electric version of the 12-string failed to take off until 1964, when George Harrison invented a new, jangly sound for 'A Hard Day's Night' with his Rickenbacker, and Roger McGuinn used his own instrument for 'Mr. Tambourine Man', the Byrds' first number-one single.

Fender wasted no time in responding with the Electric XII, a model that was better designed than the Rickenbacker in several respects. It was clearly more robust, thanks to Fender's rather more down-to-earth bolted-neck construction. Most importantly, however, the 12 machine heads were more accessible on its enormous headstock (nicknamed the 'hockey stick' because of its shape), and the bridge was a miracle of engineering with adjustable intonation for each string.

As far as its appearance was concerned, the Electric XII was aligned with recent offset models, such as the Jaguar, with an off-centre waist and a metal control plate. The large four-way pickup selector and a pair of small, split pickups (similar to the Precision bass) helped to give the instrument a unique look.

While the Electric XII was not a resounding success and was discontinued in 1969 (at the end of the psychedelic era, logically enough), Jimmy Page, Pete Townshend (the Who), the Velvet Underground, Tim Buckley and Eric Clapton still found a use for it. Johnny Winter even played an Electric XII on stage at Woodstock in 1969, although it was strung with only six strings.

Year of manufacture: 1965
Country: United States
Approximate resale value:
in this rare custom colour (Ice Blue Metallic)
with matching headstock, £10,000;
in standard sunburst, £5,800
Hear it on: Led Zeppelin, 'Stairway to Heaven' (1971)
Guitarist: Jimmy Page

NORMAL
VOLUME
TREBLE
BASS
INTENSITY
PRESENCE
Super Amp
FENDER ELECT. INST. CO.

# Fender
# 1954 Stratocaster

**It's hard to imagine what would have become of the electric guitar without Leo Fender. This genius inventor was responsible not just for the first solid-body model to be manufactured on an industrial scale (the Telecaster), but also for the design that defined the electric guitar and has served as a paradigm for three-quarters of the instruments that are on the market: the Stratocaster.**

•

The two feats are all the more impressive through being separated by only four years. This demonstrates just how far ahead of the pack Fender was, constantly seeking to improve and develop rather than resting on his laurels. After all, he could have stuck with making amplifiers and still deserve a place in history.

Leo did not work alone, of course, and his team, with George Fullerton, Bill Carson and Freddie Tavares all first among equals, made a massive contribution to the Stratocaster's success. The musicians from Southern California who regularly dropped into the Fullerton factory to shoot the breeze with Leo and try out his latest prototypes should not be forgotten, either. Leo often went to Western swing gigs (the style of music that was popular at the time, and a great favourite of his), and often lent his latest inventions to musicians in local bands to get a better idea of the instruments' viability.

The Stratocaster was the result of this openness to the opinions of musicians. It was a receptiveness that came without preconception, since Fender did not play the guitar himself, but it was also born of a perfectionism that meant the design of the instrument would continue to develop until the very last moment, even if that meant delaying its release.

As the name suggests, the Stratocaster is a product of the Space Age (if the futuristic, fun side that was typically Californian), its shape a definition of how an electric guitar should look. The body was chamfered at several points for optimal comfort, a shape Fender called a 'contour body'. There were three single-coil pickups and an extremely well-designed vibrato that was incorrectly labelled the 'synchronized tremolo' (tremolo is a variation in volume, as on amplifiers, whereas vibrato is a variation in pitch, as on the Strat; Fender has always mixed up the two). It would not be exaggerating to say that no one has ever come up with anything better.

Year of manufacture: 1954
Country: United States
Approximate resale value: £58,400
Hear it on: Buddy Holly, 'Peggy Sue' (1957)

# Zemaitis

**The vast majority of guitars of importance to rock music have been manufactured in the United States, but overseas artisans have played crucial roles in creating the sounds of the greatest guitar heroes. Of these, none could boast an order book as exclusive as the United Kingdom's Tony Zemaitis.**

•

Zemaitis, a London-based luthier of Lithuanian origin, began his career in the 1960s. His first creations were acoustics, in particular highly ornate 12-string guitars that found favour with such customers as Eric Clapton, George Harrison, Jimi Hendrix and Donovan. The 1970s was the decade of big rock sounds, however, so Zemaitis devoted his output to that style of instrument, starting with several orders from Ronnie Wood (guitarist with the Faces at the time, but who later played with Rod Stewart as a solo artist before joining the Rolling Stones, where he has stayed to this day). Zemaitis also took orders from Wood's bandmate Keith Richards, Marc Bolan, Peter Frampton and James Honeyman-Scott (the Pretenders), along with many lesser-known musicians.

One such was Mickie Owen, the guitarist with London punk band the Vibrators, who commissioned this six-string in 1978. It has all the classic features of a Zemaitis of the era: Les Paul-style body shape, 24-fret neck (a rarity at the time), bridge and tailpiece specially made for his instruments, and, most importantly, engraved metal plating. There is a small plate with a 'Z' logo on the headstock, a truss-rod cover with the name of the owner, and of course an enormous front plate decorated with motifs reminiscent of old-school tattoos: ornate flowers, a galleon, and the essential skull and crossbones. These plates, which were made by the artist Danny O'Brien (who had taken classes in decorating rifle butts), are truly Zemaitis's visual trademark.

Zemaitis retired in 2000 and died two years later. He rarely made more than about a dozen guitars a year, and these instruments have become highly sought-after cult objects in the world of rock.

Year of manufacture: 1978
Country: United Kingdom
Approximate resale value: £33,400
Hear it on: Faces, 'Stay with Me' (1971)
Guitarist: Ronnie Wood

VOX
A.G. ZEMAITIS
GUITAR-MAKER
ENGLAND • 1978

# Gibson
## SG Standard '61 Vibrola

**By the turn of the 1960s, Gibson was looking to reinvent itself. The Flying V and the Explorer had been dismal failures, and even the Les Paul, the company's star model, was losing its lustre. Only the Junior, the simplest and cheapest version, was enjoying some success in its latest iteration.**

•

The Les Paul Junior and the Les Paul Special began to change in shape and colour after 1958. Instead of the single-cutaway shape that had been retained for the Standard and Custom models, they acquired two curved horns, while the dark sunburst of the initial years was supplanted as the default colour by cherry red, a hue that nicely highlighted the grain of the mahogany body.

The new version of the Les Paul from 1961 was no doubt partly inspired by these developments. The model was in the process of being quietly forgotten as a relic of the previous decade, an old-style instrument a world away from flashy Fenders and Gretsches, so Gibson updated its look completely. The new Les Paul had a radically different shape, with two pointed horns, a satanic cherry-red finish and a thin mahogany body bereft of a maple cap. Taking a leaf out of the Strat's book, it was given a chamfered body and a vibrato (on the guitar shown here, the Lyre Vibrola with its enormous metal plate). The very first examples had featured the bizarre Sideways Vibrola, although the default was to become a fixed bridge, as on the old Pauls.

Les Paul himself was not a fan of the new version of his guitar, or so the story goes; in fact, he was in the middle of a divorce, and had he renewed his contract with Gibson, half of everything he made would have gone to his ex-wife. His name was removed from the Les Paul in 1963, but the new shape was retained in the catalogue under the simple name SG (solid guitar).

Year of manufacture: 2019
Country: United States
Approximate resale value: £1,300
Hear it on: AC/DC, 'You Shook Me All Night Long' (1980)
Guitarist: Angus Young

RHYTHM
TREBLE

# Gibson
# Les Paul Special

**The Les Paul Special had always been something of a middle child, tucked in somewhere between the glorious simplicity of the Junior and the sophisticated class of the Gold Top. There is much to be said in favour of this intermediate model, however, and musicians are now going back for a closer look.**

•

The Special was the last to join the Gibson family of Les Pauls, finding its place in 1955 in the wake of the original Gold Top's release in 1952 and the advent of the Junior and Custom models in 1954. In terms of features, it is closer to the Junior, with a wraparound bridge (even after 1955), P90s (even after 1957), dot fret markers and, most importantly, a body made from a block of mahogany with no maple cap. It nonetheless had two pickups, a bound fretboard and an inlaid headstock logo, like the Gold Top.

What really made the Special stand out was its TV Yellow colour. While this had been an optional extra for the Junior, the TV finish was standard on the Special. This shade of yellow had originally been called Limed Oak, then Limed Mahogany (after furniture fashionable at the time), and its transparent tint clearly showed the grain of the mahogany lurking beneath. Depending on the era and the individual guitar, it can be anything from a light flaxen yellow bordering on white, to a deep mustard colour.

The name TV Yellow remains a mystery to this day. Experts have long maintained that this shade allowed the guitar to appear perfectly white on the black-and-white televisions of the era, but professional guitarists would have gone for the prestigious Custom in any case. It may have been a reference to Fender's Telecaster, the butterscotch colour of which was very similar to TV Yellow, or simply an attempt to exploit the television exposure of the man who had given his name to the guitar. Perhaps it was all three.

Year of manufacture: 1957
Country: United States
Approximate resale value: £16,700
Hear it on: Bob Marley and the Wailers, 'No Woman, No Cry' (*Live!*, 1975)

100
Marshall

Fender

# JIM IRSAY

## THE SMAUG OF GUITARS

**Auctions of guitars that once belonged to famous artists have skyrocketed as a phenomenon since the 2000s, and such instruments now fetch insane sums. One name that crops up among collectors with a regularity that commands considerable respect is that of Jim Irsay.**

•

It all started in June 1999. Having just set up his Crossroads addiction recovery centre in Antigua, Eric Clapton sold about a hundred of his guitars through the UK auction house Christie's to finance it. He was hoping to raise US$500,000, but the auction ultimately brought in nine times that sum, including $450,000 just for his Strat 'Brownie'.

This was the moment the whole world realized that stars' guitars had become the new Eldorado. It encouraged two parallel developments: musicians beginning to view their equipment as items they could sell for enticing sums; and collectors, who had been accumulating rare and vintage guitars in excellent condition, going on the lookout for instruments with well-documented musical provenance.

It was at this moment that Jim Irsay, an Illinois native and owner of the Indianapolis Colts American football team, entered the auction game; as a billionaire, he could well afford his collecting habit. He had bought the manuscript of Jack Kerouac's novel *On the Road* (1957) in 2001, followed in 2002 by his first celebrity guitar (the Tiger owned by the Grateful Dead's Jerry Garcia). Irsay has continued to purchase instruments of indisputable historical importance, including several guitars and drum kits owned by the Beatles (in particular, George Harrison's SG), Bob Dylan's Stratocaster from the Newport Folk Festival, and the Martin played by Clapton for his *Unplugged* concert in 1992.

Guitar auctions moved to another level in 2019 with the records that were set when the collection owned by David Gilmour (Pink Floyd) was sold. Irsay bought the Black Strat for $3,975,000, an outright record for an electric guitar that he himself beat three years later when he bought Kurt Cobain's Mustang for $4,550,000. To date, Irsay's collection comprises more than 200 prestigious guitars and a host of memorabilia, with a total value in excess of $1 billion. It is yet to be displayed in a museum of its own, but Irsay regularly lends instruments to institutions and exhibitions.

# Teisco Spectrum 5

**Japanese manufacturing was long considered a poor second choice to the so-called professional guitars coming out of American factories. From the 1960s, however, models with absolutely stunning looks began to offer the usual suspects some competition.**

•

In common with much of the rest of the world, Japan fell for the charms of British-inspired pop music (that is to say, the Beatles) in the mid-1960s, resulting in a vibrant local scene with such groups as the Blue Comets and the Spacemen. Japanese domestic brands also began to carve out a niche for themselves overseas, including Yamaha (which had been manufacturing pianos for quite some time), Guyatone and Teisco.

The Japanese brands produced more-or-less faithful copies of Stratocasters and various Les Pauls, but they also set about designing original models. Many of these had an offset waist (like the Jazzmaster and Jaguar) or daring, kitschy looks that owed nothing to the heritage of the big American brands.

The Teisco Spectrum 5 has a special place among the Japanese models of the 1960s because of its distinctive, incredibly striking appearance. It took its name from the spectrum of sounds that could be dialled up via its five coloured switches (reminiscent of the buttons on a child's toy). However, with its offset shape and pointed horns, a choice of red or blue finish, colourful buttons, metal knobs, enormous vibrato, parachute-shaped fret markers and white plastic cover on the asymmetrical headstock, it was difficult to make head or tail of. Even the three pickups were divided in two to give a stereo sound, with each set of three strings routed to its own amplifier.

The Spectrum 5 fascinated the great Mark Knopfler, who sold five examples at auction in 2024: one in cream, a sunburst, two red and even a bass version. These five instruments sold for a total of about £91,000.

Year of manufacture: 1967
Country: Japan
Approximate resale value: £2,500
Hear it on: Mark Knopfler, 'True Love Will Never Fade' (2007)

Spectrum 5
5
4
3
2
1
MONO
STEREO
MONO
1
2

# Epiphone Coronet

**Vintage Epiphones are mostly known for their excellent hollow-body models (the Casino in particular) and their acoustics (the Texan), but this subsidiary of Gibson was also an early exponent of solid-body guitars in designs that were striking and original in equal measure.**

•

Solid-body Epiphones are now mostly Asian copies of Les Pauls and SGs, the star products of its parent company, Gibson. In the 1950s, however, when Gibson had just purchased its main competitor on the archtop market, Epiphone was given its own models with a view to endowing it with a distinctive personality. It was a cunning way of conjuring the impression of competition.

The Crestwood first appeared in 1958, followed by the Coronet and the Wilshire in 1959. All three had the same shape, with two rounded cutaways (like the Paul Junior of the same era, although the overall effect was not the same), and the same headstock, with the two rows of three machine heads typical of the brand. All three started life with New Yorker single coils left over from Epiphone's inventory, but the Crestwood (which also boasted a vibrato) was the only one to keep these when the other two moved over to P90s, two for the Wilshire (which had a Tune-O-Matic bridge) and one for the Coronet (which had a wraparound).

In simple terms, the Wilshire was Epiphone's SG Special, while the Coronet was its SG Junior (even if it cost $10 more than the latter at the time). Epiphone updated the model in 1963, giving it an asymmetrical body with a longer cutaway on the bass side, a nickel P90 cover to replace the black, and the famous 'batwing' headstock with six-in-line machine heads, a surefire way of telling it from a Gibson at a glance. They are to be found in a range of rare custom colours, including this Pacific Blue, which has aged to green but was originally Epiphone's take on Gibson's Pelham Blue. As the ultimate tease, you can even see the original colour at the spot where the pickguard has broken.

Year of manufacture: 1963
Country: United States
Approximate resale value: in this rare custom colour, £5,800; in standard red, £2,500
Hear it on: Humble Pie, '30 Days in the Hole' (1972)
Rhythm guitarist: Steve Marriott

# Martin
## D-18

**The Martin D-18 is the ultimate standard for acoustic guitars. Neither as sophisticated nor as highly prized as its elder sibling (the D-28), it remains a tried-and-tested, very practical instrument, reassuring and inspiring in equal measure, that has allowed the greatest to exorcise their innermost demons.**

•

The Martin D-18 appeared in the Martin catalogue at the turn of the 1930s, the same time as the D-28. It, too, became a dreadnought in 1934, with the body meeting the neck at the fourteenth fret, a shape it retains to this day. Telling the two apart is very simple: the D-28 is a little more ornate, but the principal contrast is that the back and sides of the D-28 are rosewood while the D-18 has an all-mahogany body. This difference had consequences for the appearance, the price and, above all, the sound of the D-18, which was considered brasher and more direct.

This difference has given the D-18 the status of the people's dreadnought, a guitar for songwriters, an instrument that you can take out on the road and not worry that it might suffer a few knocks. This D-18 from 1953 nicely shows the particular beauty that is revealed when an old dreadnought has so much wear that the wood of the soundboard has been hollowed out, and a piece of the rosette around the sound hole has been removed. Even the mismatched bridge pins are part of the romantic appeal of this grand old lady, which has belonged to the artists Mary Lou Lord, Elliott Smith and Kurt Cobain. It is also the guitar that is heard in the acoustic passages of Nirvana's masterpiece *Nevermind*, which has earned it the title of the 'saddest guitar of all time' (the association with Smith probably didn't hurt, either).

The D-18 is not just an instrument for gloomy singers, however; it is also the guitar of choice for bluegrass, a style of country music in which dizzying instrumental skill is the norm. Since bluegrass is played without amplification, a powerful guitar is required, and the D-18 can certainly unleash the greatest volume from a standing start; the most sonorous have been nicknamed 'cannons'.

Year of manufacture: 1953
Country: United States
Approximate resale value: £8,300
Hear it on: Nirvana, 'Something in the Way' (1991)
Guitarist: Kurt Cobain

# Gibson
# Firebird III Non-Reverse

**Although it has since become an integral part of the Gibson legend, the first Firebird lasted only two years before being re-released in 196 with the same model number but a new shape. This second version also proved to be anything but a resounding success, however.**

•

Looking back, one could get the impression that every Fender and Gibson model of the 1950s and 60s immediately established itself as a classic; they are now so much a part of the furniture. However, many enjoyed only a very short lifespan and were rediscovered later by curious musicians. The Firebird is one model that was dropped from the brand's catalogue for a considerable time and existed in its original form only from 1963 until 1965.

The reasons for the change in shape in 1965 are still unclear. Some claim that the original iteration was too similar to a Jazzmaster and that Fender was threatening Gibson with a lawsuit, but this seems highly unlikely, not least because the new shape was in fact even closer in appearance to the Fender guitar. It is not unthinkable that the manufacturing process for the new model, with its through body, was too complicated and took too long for a factory working on the scale employed at Gibson.

Whatever the reason, the new Firebird closely resembled the old, 'reversed' shape, with a longer cutaway on the bass side and the headstock the normal way round, hence the 'Non-Reverse' name. There had been considerable structural changes, since the neck was glued in rather than through the body. That aligned it more closely with the SG Junior and the Special, in particular because all these had dot fret markers and the pickups had been changed to P90s on the two cheapest models, the I (two pickups) and III (three pickups). The V and VII featured a full Lyre Vibrola vibrato, with two Firebird pickups on the former and three on the latter. The price was also much lower, but even that would not be enough to drum up customers in any numbers.

Year of manufacture: 1966
Country: United States
Approximate resale value: £4,200
Hear it on: The Rolling Stones, 'Have You Seen Your Mother, Baby, Standing in the Shadow?' (1966)
Guitarist: Brian Jones

VOLUME
TONE
TONE
VOLUME

# Rickenbacker 325/1996

**First and foremost, Rickenbacker has always been the brand of the Beatles. While many other musicians have been inspired by the instruments coming out of Santa Ana, the shadow cast by John Lennon is so long that it is impossible to ignore. No discussion of the 325 model or the 1996, its UK counterpart, is complete without a mention of the famous band.**

•

The Rickenbacker 325 was the first guitar in the Capri range, the instruments that would become the brand's visual and sonic trademark. These successors to the solid-body Combo were semi-hollow, although this was not immediately apparent on the very first models. On Lennon's two main 325s (one with a natural finish and one in black), no sound hole is visible on the top, and you might well imagine they had solid bodies.

The superb design of the 325 was the work of Roger Rossmeisl, a German luthier's son who went on to work at Fender, and it was an instrument with the very short scale length of 52.7cm (20¾in). Rickenbacker initially launched it as a three-quarter-size instrument, which may have been what won Lennon over when he bought it in Hamburg. He modified it by swapping the knobs, installing a Bigsby vibrato to replace the original Vibrola, and disconnecting the middle pickup (the guitar has three). These pickups are in fact single-coil, despite the two black apertures in the chrome – a look that earned them the nickname 'toasters' because of how they looked when viewed from above. John Fogerty replaced his 325's bridge toaster with a Gibson humbucker, and this is what can be heard on most Creedence Clearwater Revival tracks.

It is difficult enough to work out which Rickenbacker model is which because they are classified only by number, but the guitars imported to the United Kingdom add a further layer of complexity. The distributor, Rose-Morris, decided to make up its own designations, and the 325 was rebranded the 1996 for the local market.

Year of manufacture: 1964
Country: United States
Approximate resale value: £7,500
Hear it on: The Beatles, 'I Want to Hold Your Hand' (1964)
Guitarist: John Lennon

# Gretsch
## White Falcon

**Gretsch has never been a brand for shy and retiring guitarists, and this is doubly true in the case of the famous White Falcon. Since the moment of its creation in 1954, no guitar has been as eye-catching or ornate as this famous bird, and in this respect, it represents the childhood dreams of many a guitar hero. That has allowed it to find favour with big names from a wide variety of music styles.**

•

From Neil Young to Malcolm Young (AC/DC), from Billy Duffy (the Cult) to John Frusciante (Red Hot Chili Peppers), and from James Hetfield to Lady Gaga, the White Falcon has become the guitar of choice for radically different musicians, whether for a brief appearance or a long-term association.

The White Falcon (model number 6136) was never originally planned as an addition to the Gretsch catalogue, however. The musician Jimmie Webster (who managed the brand's marketing) wanted to raise its profile at the NAMM (National Association of Music Merchants) show in 1954, so he designed a completely over-the-top instrument as a one-off to display on the Gretsch stand and showcase what they could do. As such, he indulged in every possible excess, with gold hardware nicely set off by the white finish, a vertical headstock logo, large fret marker inlays and – particularly special – triple binding around the body, the F-holes, the fretboard and the headstock. The gold sparkle fretboard binding was an idea borrowed from the division of Gretsch that looked after its drum kits.

The trouble was that the dealers loved it and placed orders for the new model, even though it was priced at a whopping US$600 (at a time when the extremely high-end Les Paul Custom cost $360). It was an outlandish amount for an outlandish guitar. The White Falcon has since become Gretsch's iconic model, embodying the brand and its penchant for visual excess. This magnificent Falcon, fitted with the Dynasonic/DeArmond pickups that are typical for pre-1957 Falcons, belongs to Frusciante.

Year of manufacture: 1955
Country: United States
Approximate resale value: £83,400
Hear it on: The Cult, 'She Sells Sanctuary' (1985)
Guitarist: Billy Duffy

GRETSCH
Bigsby
PATENT
No.D-169,120

# Gretsch Custom Shop Blue Penguin

**The Gretsch Custom Shop makes guitars almost exclusively to order. Many are visually spectacular instruments, such as this incredible Penguin. It is not a replica of a vintage guitar – far from it, in fact – but that's the whole point.**

•

Gretsch's history is more than a little chequered. Its takeover by Baldwin in 1967 ushered in an obvious drop in quality, and two fires at its Arkansas factory finally put paid to the brand, which halted production in 1981. The Gretsch family were down but not out, however. Fred Gretsch (great-nephew of the brand's founder), along with his wife, Dinah, bought back the company in 1984 and restarted guitar production in Japan in 1989. A partnership with Fender in 2002 brought Gretsch back on course, and the first American Gretsch for 23 years finally rolled off the production line in 2004, manufactured in what was to become the brand's Custom Shop under the aegis of Senior Master Builder Stephen Stern.

In Fender Custom Shop terminology, a Master Builder is a particularly skilled luthier who makes guitars from start to finish (rather than concentrating on one particular task), and appends his or her signature to the instrument in question when it is finished. There is thus a difference between team-built guitars, made by a group in a small workshop, and master-built examples, where a single artisan is responsible for the entire process.

Gretsch's Custom Shop may be housed on the same premises as Fender, but it is a much smaller workshop and handles far fewer orders. All Gretsch Custom Shop guitars are master-built instruments that have been designed by their future owners, rather than short-run models.

This commission for Scott Holiday (Rival Sons) references the White Penguin design from the late 1950s, but with three pickups, chrome hardware, an armrest, a Bigsby vibrato and, of course, a blue sparkle finish that gives the most beautiful effect. It is anything but faithful to the vintage model, but that should not be allowed to spoil the pleasure it gives.

Year of manufacture: 2010s
Country: United States
Approximate resale value: £4,200
Hear it on: Rival Sons, 'Too Bad' (2019)
Guitarist: Scott Holiday

GRETSCH
GRETSCH
BY
Bigsby

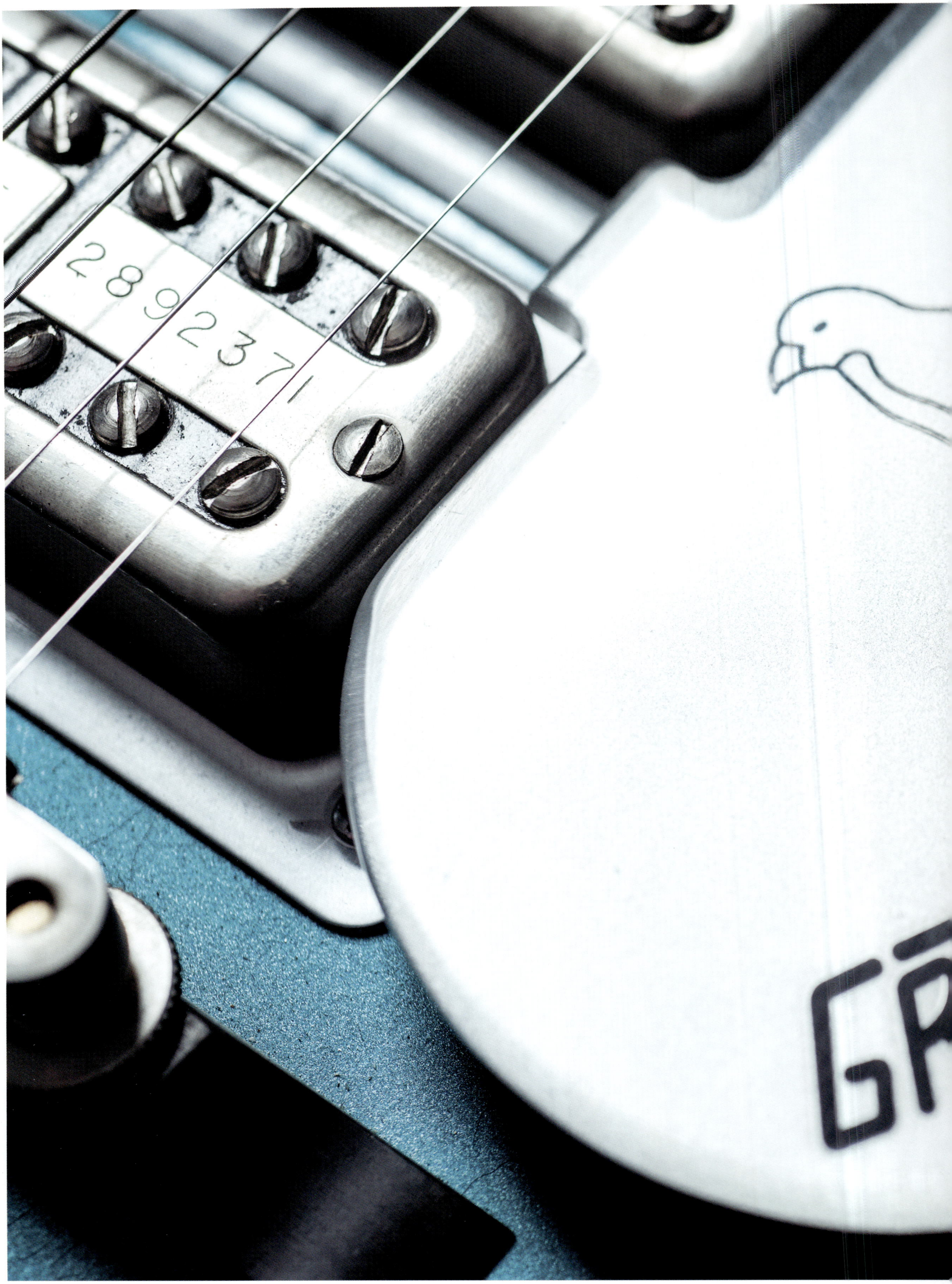

**Gretsch Blue Penguin**
Gretsch's scratchplates are as ornate as its guitars; the Chet Atkins models feature his emblem and the White Falcon sports the raptor after which the model was named. Logically enough, the scratchplate of the Penguin bears an image of the bird in question, here slightly worn away alongside scratches in the plastic that may have been part of the original ageing process.

# Fender Custom Colour Stratocaster

**There's nothing like a beautiful colour to showcase the exceptionally graceful shape of a Stratocaster. The design is a perfect union of ergonomics and elegance, and remains to this day the shape that non-guitarists call to mind whenever the electric guitar is mentioned.**

•

The default sunburst finish that was made available did not necessarily show off the Strat to its best advantage, however. While the Les Paul and ES-335 had been aligned with the archtops of the 1930s (where you could have any colour you liked as long as it was sunburst), and the Telecaster lent itself readily to a spartan, functional finish showcasing the grain of the wood, the Stratocaster was another kind of instrument altogether. Long before the Jazzmaster or Jaguar, it was the guitar of the future and the first to turn heads with its elegant, avant-garde curves. This guitar was one to haunt the dreams of a thousand guitarists with their noses pressed to the shop windows of the 1960s, an era in which it was impossible to find a decent copy at a reasonable price.

Essentially, the aerodynamic, Space Age, typically Californian shape of the Stratocaster was a shoo-in for solid colours that did not show the wood beneath. You don't see metal under the paint job of a car, and the Stratocaster was like a Cadillac: not only a functional item, but also an object of fascination that was to become a holy relic in its own right.

This superb example was manufactured in 1964, less than a year before Fender was bought out by CBS, after which there was a considerable drop in instrument quality. As such, it is already highly sought-after as a pre-CBS custom-colour guitar, not least because it was ordered with gold hardware, making it incredibly rare. The colour in question was known as Inca Silver Metallic, a shade used on Chevrolet Corvettes in the late 1950s and picked up by Fender between 1960 and 1965 before being replaced by Firemist Silver, a colour used by...Cadillac – and so the torch was passed on.

Year of manufacture: 1964
Country: United States
Approximate resale value: £41,700
Hear it on: Robert Cray, 'Blues Get Off My Shoulder' (2012)

NORMAL
VOLUME
TREBLE
BASS
TREBLE
SPEED
INTENSITY
Vibroverb
Amp
FENDER ELECT. INST. CO.
DESIGN & CIRCUITS
PATENTED
Fender
VOLUME
TONE
TONE

# Gibson
## Firebird V

**Some portion of the history of Gibson's electric models can be explained in the light of competition from Fender and the Kalamazoo brand's desire to challenge the sun-drenched shapes coming out of California. After the failure of the Flying V and the Explorer, the Firebird was a further attempt to pursue this course.**

•

In 1962 Ted McCarty decided to bet the farm on a design commissioned from a virtuoso in the field. He contacted Ray Dietrich, a renowned (but retired) car designer, and convinced him to work on a guitar shape for the first time. The outcome was reminiscent of an Explorer but softer and more compact, with a treble horn longer than the one on the bass side. That feature gained it the sobriquet 'reverse', since it was more common (and more logical) for the bass horn to be longer than the treble.

The new model was called the Firebird (the eponymous car would not appear until 1967), symbolizing Gibson's renaissance after its all-too-rapid relegation to the ranks of a brand for senescent jazz guitarists. The construction was as radical as the design, with a through neck made of nine strips of mahogany and walnut, banjo-style machine heads so that they didn't stick out beyond the headstock (which was also reversed), and pickups that looked similar to Epiphone's mini humbuckers but were in fact a new design with no visible pole pieces, offering a bright, cutting sound.

Four models were available: the single-pickup Firebird I, with a wraparound bridge and dot fret markers (the Junior of the series); the Firebird III, with two pickups and a rudimentary vibrato; the twin-pickup V (pictured), with 'crown' fret markers and a full Lyre Vibrola vibrato; and the VII, with three pickups and Custom-style markers. The Firebird was also the first Gibson model to be made available in ten custom colours, including the superb Cardinal Red seen here.

Year of manufacture: 1964
Country: United States
Approximate resale value:
in this very rare custom colour and with provenance from Brian Ray, £83,400;
in standard sunburst, £10,000
Hear it on: Johnny Winter, 'It's All Over Now' (*Captured Live!*, 1976)

# B C Rich
## Eagle

**Since the late 1960s some luthiers have sought to elevate the building of electric guitars to a major art form, unburdened by the constraints of large-scale production or the need to make a profit. Using the finest possible materials, they have also defined the boundaries of the ultimate version of the instrument, and we experience their legacy to this day.**

•

The late 1960s were an era of experimentation in both music and materials. Groups emerging from the American wave of psychedelia in particular were set on new sonic adventures and worked in close collaboration with the luthiers and electronic engineers who were capable of following them into the delirium of their imaginations.

Bernardo Chavez Rico started making electric guitars in Los Angeles in 1968, although his brand truly began to take off only in the 1970s. The Eagle model, released in 1976, was the second to be designed by the B C Rich workshop after the Seagull (and continued the ornithological theme).

The Eagle is the perfect embodiment of Rico's insistence on excellence at every level. The maple neck is a 'through' design, which is to say that it extends to form the central section of the body, with a wing of highly figured maple attached to each side. This was a fiddly and expensive process, since everything was done by hand. The hardware is also of its time: the bridge is a Badass (the result of some hard work by two repairers hoping to achieve the best possible intonation) and the pickups are by DiMarzio, a brand established in 1972 by New Yorker Larry DiMarzio, who had hit upon the idea of selling replacement pickups with a much higher output than the Gibsons of the time. The two Super Distortion pickups are routed through a complex circuit of preamplifiers and switches designed by the electronic engineer Neal Moser.

These luxurious instruments have found favour with a host of musicians, from Aerosmith to Guns N' Roses, and B C Rich has become one of the most fashionable brands in the world of metal.

Year of manufacture: 1978
Country: United States
Approximate resale value: £4,200
Hear it on: Guns N' Roses, 'You Could Be Mine' (1991)
Guitarist: Slash

100

finding the best ways to economize on production costs to increase margins. They enforced cheese-paring savings (on screws, for example) as well as more wide-ranging changes, in particular to the quality of wood reserves. That subsequently took a nosedive, resulting in instruments that were far too heavy (although it should be noted that the old, properly air-dried stocks had already been exhausted by the post-1964 boom in demand).

To address this problem, Fender hit on a brilliant idea: to hollow out the body of the guitar to make it lighter, much as Gretsch had done with the Duo Jet a dozen years earlier. They excavated the part of the Telecaster hidden beneath the scratchplate so that the modification would remain invisible, giving rise to the infamous Smuggler's Tele of 1967 (the idea presumably being that it was possible to secrete contraband in the cavity of the guitar).

In 1968 Fender took this procedure to its logical conclusion, and it was the designer Roger Rossmeisl (him again) who designed the elegant Thinline Telecaster. His idea was to hollow out the upper part of the body and showcase this with a single F-hole, but to make the design slicker, the scratchplate also had to be reshaped.

At the time, the Thinline was available in ash or mahogany, two options that were called Groovy Naturals in the catalogue in an attempt to couch things in hippy terms. This blend of natural finishes and pearloid scratchplates defined the look of 1970s Fenders, and – for better or worse – many other brands took inspiration from it.

Year of manufacture: 1968
Country: United States
Approximate resale value: £12,500
Hear it on: Carole King, 'It's Too Late' (1971)
Guitarist: Danny Kortchmar

FENDER

# Gibson
## J-45

**Big brands have often tried to copy one another's homework, but because of their radically different cultures, the resulting instruments have opened up new horizons with their own look and sound, irrespective of the original inspiration.**

•

During the 1930s, the time of the Great Depression, Gibson was selling the J-35 model, and it would become the J-45 in 1942. At that time Gibson was not supposed to be manufacturing guitars, the materials having been requisitioned for the war effort. Despite everything, the factory continued to operate, producing guitars made exclusively by women because all the men had been called up.

The change in model number was principally a change in price, and the J-45 took its name from the US$45 that was required if you wished to buy one at the time (the equivalent of £750 today). The letter J stands for Jumbo, denoting a round-shouldered version of the Martin dreadnought. Martin's D-18 was in fact considerably more expensive (at $65), but the two guitars had similar features, with a Sitka spruce top and mahogany back, sides and neck. Martin's fretboards were ebony (as opposed to the rosewood used by Gibson), and sunburst finishes, which were the norm at Gibson, were very rare and much lighter at Martin. The J-45 was also available in a natural finish, but this was more expensive, a fact that clearly shows how practical the dark sunburst was for hiding defects in the appearance of the wood used for the soundboard. Gibson's approach to manufacturing simply did not insist on the same excellence as that required of Martin employees.

Over all the years since its launch, and through all the artists who have made it their guitar of choice, the J-45 (which is still in production) has established a raw sound of its own. Dark and rounded, it is the perfect accompaniment to the voices of such singers as Bruce Springsteen, Bob Dylan, Buddy Holly, Woody Guthrie and Gillian Welch.

Year of manufacture: 1959
Country: United States
Approximate resale value: £6,700
Hear it on: James Taylor, 'Fire and Rain' (1970)

# James Trussart
## Steelcaster

**James Trussart is one of those rare luthiers who have managed to create a new aesthetic in their own right, an immediately identifiable style that no one else has truly mastered. He is also the only French practitioner to have carved out a niche for himself among American guitarists.**

•

French by birth, certainly, but American by choice, James Trussart was born in Lorraine, a stone's throw from the borders with Germany, Belgium and Luxembourg. After a first career spent playing Cajun violin and making guitars in the Pigalle district of Paris, he left for Los Angeles in 2000, at the age of 50. Since then, his superb workshop has become a meeting place for the greatest musicians from California and farther afield. It was through Trussart's intervention, for example, that Bob Dylan recruited a number of musicians for his band.

Trussart's guitars are noted for their use of steel. He works the metal to make the bodies of his guitars and plays with the textures that are created when it wears, even incorporating rust into his process. The shape of the Steelcaster is obviously lifted from the Telecaster, but Trussart's approach makes it an instrument in its own right. The body of this example is not made entirely of steel; rather, it is one of his more recent instruments, for which a wooden body (made of sugar pine) has been hollowed out to accept a steel plate. From the back, you could almost believe that it is a traditional guitar, but from the front, the steel with its snakeskin patterning (a natural process that takes several days) leaves you in no doubt about the identity of the luthier.

Trussart guitars have found favour with musicians as varied as Tom Morello (Rage Against the Machine), Joe Perry (Aerosmith) and Joe Gore (Tom Waits). Each instrument is so striking in appearance that it invariably becomes a central feature of its owner's stage arsenal.

Year of manufacture: 2010s
Country: United States
Approximate resale value: £3,300
Hear it on: DJ Shadow, 'Broken Levee Blues' (2006)
Guitarist: Joe Gore

INTENSITY

**James Trussart**
The headstock of this Trussart demonstrates the same attention to detail as the rest of the guitar. There is a wooden surround with a metal plate decorated with a snake motif, and the logo has been cut out of the plate to reveal the metal mesh below. Similarly, opting for vintage-style machine heads is a crucial aesthetic choice.

# Gibson
## Les Paul Custom

**The idea of a range of guitars derived from an initial model was yet to become the norm in the 1950s. Gibson even created a new model number for the ES-295 in 1952, despite the fact that it was no more than an ES-175 in a different finish. The advent of the Les Paul Custom in 1954 heralded a radical change to this way of seeing things.**

•

The original Les Paul model met with considerable success when it was launched in 1952, helped both by the media exposure of Les Paul the musician and by Gibson's reputation for quality. In 1954 the company's CEO, Ted McCarty, was inspired to exploit a fashion prevalent in the car industry whereby several versions of the same car model would commonly be available; this was not yet the case in the world of guitars, but the Les Paul was set to be released as both an entry-level variant and a higher-quality model.

A price list dating from 1955 features the Les Paul Junior at US$110, the Les Paul Model (the original Gold Top) at $235 and the Custom for $360 – more than three times the price of the Junior. Paul viewed the Custom as a beautiful stage prop (hence its black colour and the nickname Black Beauty), and he wanted very low frets so that he could play faster, hence its other nickname, the Fretless Wonder. It also has every possible decoration: gold hardware (including even the pickup pole pieces and the Bigsby, as on the example shown here), binding on the front and back of the body as well as along the fretboard and around the headstock, block fret markers, and a split diamond logo on the headstock.

Structurally, the Custom has a carved, solid mahogany body with no maple cap, and this beautiful guitar was the first Les Paul to be fitted with the new Tune-O-Matic bridge right from its release (the Gold Top would upgrade its bridge the following year). When Gibson invented the humbucking pickup in 1957, the Custom was given three of them, as seen on this 1958 beauty of unparalleled class.

Year of manufacture: 1958
Country: United States
Approximate resale value: £83,400
Hear it on: Peter Frampton, 'Do You Feel Like We Do'
(*Frampton Comes Alive!*, 1976)

Bigsby
PATENT

# Gibson
# 1959 Les Paul Standard

**Two Les Paul Standards (models from 1958 and 1960) have already featured in this book (on pages 62 and 24, respectively), but the undisputed Holy Grail status of the Burst means that we must also examine this example from 1959. It's undoubtedly the most sought-after year for the Les Paul Standard, and this simple form embodies all the fantasies that surround Gibson's most famous guitar.**

•

Every Burst is unique, and this is also what makes them so fascinating for collectors. The patterns formed by the grain of the two-piece maple cap mean that the top of each guitar is effectively like an identity card. These patterns may be tiger-striped, flamed, bird's-eye or even very understated (the famous plain tops), but it is always easy to identify the guitar you are dealing with, even from a black-and-white photo. Combine this with the fact that the red of the sunburst finish tended to fade with exposure to UV light and you have a palette of possible colours, depending on the life the instrument has lived.

Les Paul Standards from 1958 and 1960 are highly prized, but the 1959 is surely the most attractive, and has been the guitar of choice for such great Burst players as Jimmy Page, Billy Gibbons, Peter Green, Duane Allman and Keith Richards. It is indeed the perfect transition model, with a neck thinner than the '58 but thicker than the '60, a red finish that does not stay too red (unlike the '60), and fat frets that are more agreeable to play on than the too-narrow frets of the '58. These tiny adjustments have made the '59 the 'Goldilocks' Les Paul, in that it is just right.

The magnificent example shown here, dating to 1960, has ambered beautifully over the years, and its maple cap is superbly flamed. Known as the BI (most Bursts have a nickname, and their serial numbers are well known), it has been played by Joe Bonamassa, Marcus King and Tommy Emmanuel.

Year of manufacture: 1959
Country: United States
Approximate resale value: £250,200
Hear it on: Led Zeppelin, 'Heartbreaker' (1969)
Guitarist: Jimmy Page

# Fender
# Blackguard Telecaster

**Even today, the Telecaster remains a symbol of the guitar as a tool par excellence, the instrument of true musicians with no need for bells and whistles to find the sound they want. Certain styles of playing have even come about because of the features of this model, which continues to fascinate more than 70 years after its first appearance.**

•

When Leo Fender received Gretsch's letter asking him to rename his Broadcaster, he stuck with the world of broadcasting and media by plumping for television, the latest novelty in the business. It was another visionary decision. In 1950 no more than 9 per cent of American households boasted a television set (which would have been black and white, of course), but by 1959 this figure would soar to 85 per cent. In much the same way, the industry initially scoffed at this solid-body guitar, which was nicknamed the 'plank' when it was launched, but the Telecaster has become an essential and iconic instrument.

The Telecasters from this first era exert a special fascination. The instruments produced between 1952 and 1955 originally had identical features, but ageing has endowed each with a very particular personality. The original colour was a transparent yellow that showed off the grain of the swamp ash then used for the body (a hue nicknamed Butterscotch Blonde, which was the only option available). Inspired by the logic of Henry Ford and his 'any colour you like, as long as it's black' approach, Leo Fender elected not to offer any alternatives for this model, thereby making production as streamlined as possible. It was the black Bakelite scratchplate hiding the pickup wiring that gave these early instruments the nickname Blackguard, and these simple guitars have inspired millions of musicians, from country to hard rock.

Year of manufacture: 1953
Country: United States
Approximate resale value: £50,000
Hear it on: The Rolling Stones, 'Start Me Up' (1981)
Guitarist: Keith Richards

EXCELSIOR

# Epiphone
## Texan

**Some guitars will always be associated with one particular artist, model or even song, and if the track in question is sufficiently well known and historically important, the guitar linked with it can become legendary in its own right. This has clearly been the case for the Epiphone Texan.**

•

By 1964 Beatlemania was at its peak; the Beatles were the most famous celebrities in the world and every note they played was snapped up, analysed and adored by millions. Up to this point, Paul McCartney, the band's bass player, had exclusively been using his Höfner 500/1 (the violin bass), but at the end of 1964 he bought himself two guitars, one electric and one acoustic. The former was a Casino and the latter a Texan, both made by Epiphone, the American brand that had been bought by Gibson seven years earlier.

McCartney had just finished composing a new song while shooting the film *Help!* at the turn of 1965, and decided to record it alone, accompanying himself on his Epiphone Texan. The result was 'Yesterday', both the first song to be recorded by a solo Beatle and one of the most famous pop songs of all time. *Guinness World Records* lists it as the most frequently covered song ever recorded, and it is also one of the most played songs in radio history. Put another way, it is a phenomenon bigger even than the Beatles, a truly historic event.

The modest Epiphone Texan was also known as the FT-79, a model number that Epiphone had used as early as 1942, although for a very different instrument. When Gibson bought the brand in 1957, it turned most of Epiphone's instruments into close cousins of Gibsons, and the Texan acquired a family resemblance to the J-45, with a long scale length and slightly different look. Because of its association with Macca and 'Yesterday', however, the Epiphone version has become much more sought-after.

Year of manufacture: 1965
Country: United States
Approximate resale value: £5,000
Hear it on: The Beatles, 'Yesterday' (1965)
Guitarist: Paul McCartney

Explorer

# Fender
## Musicmaster

**The second half of the 1950s was the era of the beginner. This was the moment when the big brands realized that it was in their interest to become involved in the market for entry-level guitars, otherwise they would be left in the dust by other manufacturers making it their focus.**

•

Nathan Daniel launched Danelectro guitars in 1954 with the aim of selling instruments that would be accessible to all while sacrificing as little as possible in terms of manufacturing quality and sound. They were all produced in the United States and benefited greatly from a strong presence in national department stores. Gibson started to take an interest in this market when it launched the Les Paul Junior the same year, so it was only logical that Fender should throw its hat into the ring.

The Californian brand was undoubtedly slower out of the traps for a couple of reasons. For a start, it was firing on all cylinders at the time, and it is easy to imagine that developing models as revolutionary as the Telecaster, followed by the Precision Bass and the Stratocaster, took up all of the company's time and energy. In addition, Fender guitars were already relatively affordable thanks to their simplicity of design and production-line assembly.

Fender eventually responded with the Musicmaster in 1956, a charming design reminiscent of a mini-Strat despite its rock-bottom price of US$120. It came in a Desert Sand (beige) finish that was unique to this model, and featured a single pickup with a cream-coloured cover and an anodized gold scratchplate that would crop up again two years later on the Jazzmaster. The neck was the most important detail: tiny, with a scale length of 55.9cm (22in) rather than the usual 64.8cm (25½in).

Right from the start, Fender also sold a slightly more expensive dual-pickup version known as the Duo-Sonic. It proved a great success, and the two models were given an upgraded shape in 1964 before being complemented with a Duo-Sonic fitted with a vibrato that was dubbed the Mustang. All these models have had their particular fans, including such legendary musicians as Patti Smith, David Byrne (Talking Heads) and Kurt Cobain.

Year of manufacture: 1957
Country: United States
Approximate resale value: £2,500
Hear it on: Liz Phair, 'Why Can't I?' (2003)

Super Amp
BASS INSTRUMENT
VOLUME
TREBLE
BASS
PRESENCE
Fender
Fender
RON

John Mayer is one of the most iconic guitarists of the 2000s, bringing with him a rediscovery of the blues – a Stevie Ray Vaughan for a new generation. He is also a polarizing personality who annoys and entices in equal measure. For long a voluble proponent of the Stratocaster, he had a signature model between 2005 and 2014 before heading to PRS and its massively expensive, luxury models.

In 2018, however, Mayer and Paul Reed Smith unveiled the Silver Sky, a revised and updated Strat model for the general public. It featured a two-horn body with a slightly modified shape, three single coils inspired by vintage pickups, a 1963 neck profile with an 18.4cm (7¼in) fretboard radius, and a vibrato entirely in the spirit of the original.

The three-a-side machine heads would certainly come as a shock to many people, however. The launch of the Silver Sky was well publicized, not least because both PRS and Mayer cleverly built up the suspense before it was released, and it clearly shows the extent to which the online buzz has become an integral part of the launch of an instrument. Had Instagram existed in 1954, you could bet your bottom dollar that there would have been musicians going wild with accusations that Fender had designed a weird guitar that looked like nothing on earth. The Silver Sky has thus been the subject of memes and impassioned debate between fans who see it as the apotheosis of the Strat and detractors who thought the Strat was already perfect as it was. The ultimate winner was PRS, of course, since the guitar monopolized attention and became a bestseller.

This Silver Sky was one of the very first to be produced. Its Horizon Red finish was inspired by the Tesla catalogue, a nice nod to the world of automobiles that inspired Fender back in the day, but making use of its 21st-century equivalent.

Year of manufacture: 2018
Country: United States
Approximate resale value: £1,500
Hear it on: John Mayer, 'Last Train Home' (2021)

SILVER SKY
JOHN MAYER MODEL

# Epiphone
## Casino

**Most 1960s Epiphone models were minimally altered versions of instruments in the Gibson range, although the corresponding Gibson model usually had a slightly better reputation. Usually, but not always – the Epiphone Casino is a perfect counter-example.**

•

The Casino was launched in 1961 and, like the Gibson ES-330 from which it is clearly derived, is a quarter-body guitar with no centre block. It looks like an ES-335, being thin with two cutaways, but from a structural perspective it has more in common with the brand's jazz archtops. While the ES-330 has spent a long time in the doldrums as a model of little interest to the people at Gibson, the Casino has become an object of fascination for baby boomers.

The reason for this is not complicated: it was one of the Beatles' favourite guitars, and, for two of the band, their favourite guitar of all. Although George Harrison quickly moved on to other things after using it for the 'Hello Goodbye' video, John Lennon made it his weapon of choice in the group's last years, even going through two different finishes (the original sunburst, followed by a natural finish after their passage to India), and it is in this latter form that it can be seen throughout the *Get Back* documentary of 2021. Paul McCartney was the first of the band to pick up a Casino, and he is still playing it today, making this a love story that has lasted almost 60 years. Factor in Keith Richards wielding one as the Rolling Stones were breaking through and it is easy to understand how the Casino became the ultimate symbol of the British Invasion.

This example from 1967 has retained its original Pelham Blue finish. It was a typical custom colour for Gibsons, but it makes this instrument extremely rare compared with a Casino in standard sunburst.

Year of manufacture: 1967
Country: United States
Approximate resale value: in standard sunburst finish, £5,000;
in this extremely rare finish, £8,300
Hear it on: The Beatles, 'Don't Let Me Down' (1969)
Guitarist: John Lennon

VOLUME
VOLUME
TONE
TONE

# JIMI HENDRIX

## THE METEORITE

**Of all the musicians who have revolutionized the instrument, one guitarist stands head and shoulders above the rest, and still, more than half a century after his death, nothing comes close to the mystery of Jimi Hendrix. His playing has never been equalled and he continues to influence generation after generation.**

•

Despite his colossal reputation, it could be argued that Hendrix is underrated, given the extent of his talent. His flamboyant, spectacular side, with all the tricks and acrobatics, is often emphasized, to the extent that for a long time he was – to those not in the know, at least – 'that guitarist who plays with his teeth'. He was also a sonic genius, however, a musician of great sensitivity, an entirely competent singer and a great songwriter.

James Marshall Hendrix was born in Seattle in 1942 and had by the turn of the 1960s started as a sideman to artists on the Chitlin' Circuit, the concert venues that catered to Black audiences during the era of segregation. He played with the Isley Brothers and Little Richard before unveiling his solo project in New York in 1966.

No prophet is accepted in his own country, however, and Hendrix settled in London on the advice of his new manager, the Animals bassist Chas Chandler. It was the latter who put together the Jimi Hendrix Experience trio, with two British musicians, and Hendrix became the new sensation on the London scene. Word soon spread after his first single, 'Hey Joe', his first album and his incendiary performance at the Monterey Pop Festival in 1967.

Hendrix was now a superstar in the United States as well, and he pushed his experiments in sound to the limit on the next few albums, in particular on the double *Electric Ladyland* (1968). He was the first to mistreat the Stratocaster by running it through a fuzzbox into a Marshall stack, and the first to fully explore the new possibilities offered by effects pedals, such as the wah-wah and Uni-Vibe.

After his iconic appearance to close the Woodstock festival in 1969, Hendrix formed a new trio, Band of Gypsys, who played in a funkier, almost jazzy style. Unfortunately, his premature death in September 1970 prevented him from continuing in this new direction, and we can but dream of the forms his music might have taken if the Hendrix shooting star had been able to stay with us for a few more years.

# Martin Ditson
## 111 Dreadnaught

**The history of the guitar at the turn of the 20th century is a litany of attempts to reach ever higher volumes to allow the instrument to be heard. No innovation contributed as much to this arms race as the Ditson Dreadnaught.**

•

Ditson was a chain of music shops with branches in Boston, New York and Philadelphia, and, like many at the time, it was looking for ways to bring the guitar more volume. Small acoustic models were being buried by the brass of contemporary big bands, and even had their work cut out in fights against such instruments as the banjo and the mandolin. In 1915 Ditson commissioned the Martin brand to design them the era's largest guitar, an imposing beast that inherited the name Dreadnaught (a spelling that was later corrected to Dreadnought) from a line of British warships launched about ten years earlier.

The Martin Ditson was created in three formats, designated simply 1, 11 and 111 from the smallest to the largest. The 111 format was later adopted by Martin under the name Dreadnought, creating a norm that has evolved very little in more than a century.

This example from 1929 dates back to a time when acoustic guitars still had the neck joint at the twelfth fret, before the fourteenth became the norm. The shoulders of the Ditson Dreadnought are thus longer than those on the current version of this shape, creating sides that are even larger and more imposing. This layout also situates the bridge in the centre of the soundboard, an ideal location for resonance. All the stars are aligned to give the Dreadnought the most powerful voice possible.

Year of manufacture: 1929
Country: United States
Approximate resale value: £20,900
Hear it on: Norman Blake, 'Richland Avenue Rag' (1972)

# Gretsch
## 6128 Duo Jet

**The fashion for solid-body guitars was started by Fender with the Broadcaster in 1950, but the other big companies also did their bit, with each brand retaining its own personality. Gretsch's contribution was none other than the legendary Duo Jet.**

•

Copying between brands was not yet a thing in the 1950s, or at least there were no identical replicas. Similarities could be found and inspiration suspected without detracting in the slightest from the inherent merits and personality of each guitar. So when Fender released its Broadcaster (later the Telecaster) in 1950, the first mass-produced electric solid-body guitar, it was Gibson's initial inspiration to design a far more refined and aesthetically classic version in the Les Paul of 1952.

In 1953 it was Gretsch's turn to offer an interpretation: the 6128 Duo Jet. 'Duo' because it had two pickups, and 'Jet' because it was a speedy, elegant machine. With its unique, rounded cutaway, the shape was reminiscent of the Les Paul from the outset, and there is even some overlap structurally, with a carved maple cap on a mahogany body and a glued-in mahogany neck. In reality, however, the Duo Jet has a well-kept secret; it is not really a solid-body at all. It is in fact semi-solid (or semi-hollow, logically enough), with cavities in the body that are covered by the cap. Because there are no sound holes, there is nothing to indicate this internal architecture, but it has a lot to do with the Duo Jet's sonic personality, which is brighter and airier than that of the Les Paul. The DeArmond Dynasonic pickups are also very different from Gibson's P90, even though they are also single coils.

The Duo Jet was the choice of the legendary rockabilly guitarist Cliff Gallup. That, in turn, encouraged fans as illustrious as George Harrison and Jeff Beck to give it a spin.

Year of manufacture: 1956
Country: United States
Approximate resale value: £8,300
Hear it on: Gene Vincent, 'Race with the Devil' (1958)
Guitarist: Cliff Gallup

GRETSCH

# Guild
# M-75 Aristocrat

**Guild had been in existence for scarcely two years in 1954, but the New York brand was already wondering how it might contribute to the conversation about solid-body guitars. As was so often the case with Guild, it hit upon a design quite unlike anything anyone else was doing: the M-75 Aristocrat.**

•

t was Fender that opened the floodgates with its solid-body Broadcaster ir 950, followed by Gibson with the Les Paul in 1952, essentially a more refinec ersion of the design, with a carved maple cap on a mahogany body anc glued-in neck. Gretsch followed suit the next year with the Duo Jet, inventing he notion of a 'semi-solid' guitar, that is to say, one with a hollow mahogany ody topped with a maple cap.

n 1954 Guild was still striving to carve out a niche for itself. Having recruitec number of former Epiphone employees who had no wish to up sticks wher piphone moved to Philadelphia, Guild had established its workshop ir Manhattan loft. Geographically, then, only one bridge separated it from Brooklyn, home of the Gretsch factory. It was therefore logical for Guild tc adopt a semi-solid design for its M-75 Aristocrat model, but with a spruce cap which gave a radically different sound. This was much more a return to the worlc of archtop acoustics, shifting the emphasis back to the resonance of the hollow body, rather than its amplified sound.

he Aristocrat was still an electric guitar, of course. Although its two pickups esembled the cream-coloured soap-bar P90s fitted to the Les Paul Gold Top hey were in fact made by the New York brand Franz, with a lower output tha gave a softer and less aggressive sound than the Les Paul.

rom an aesthetic perspective, the Aristocrat lives up to its name with the decorative details that were reserved for the Custom model at Gibson: golc hardware, block fret markers and even an inlaid headstock (the pattern or this model from the end of the 1950s was known as the Chesterfield because t resembled the logo of that cigarette brand). The M-75 was never massively successful, however, fated to remain an obscure, cool model for fans o ohn Lee Hooker.

Year of manufacture: 1959
Country: United States
Approximate resale value: £3,300
Hear it on: The Raconteurs, 'Salute Your Solution' (2008)
Guitarist: Brendan Benson

# Fender
## Bass VI

**Not every instrument created by Fender has enjoyed the meteoric success of the Telecaster or the Precision Bass. However, they all serve as a reminder that it is not so long ago that the guitars we now consider classics were merely novelties, experiments and trials that musicians have subsequently made their own.**

•

Put simply, Fender invented the electric bass guitar. Before 1951 and the Precision Bass, there was the double bass, with its colossal dimensions and fretless neck (hence the term 'precision' to describe the intonation of notes on a neck with frets), which was extremely fiddly to amplify. Fender applied its solid-body electric guitar design to a four-string version tuned an octave lower, and the electric bass was born. Indeed, for a long time, musicians' album credits would list them as playing the 'Fender bass', rather than just bass.

Danelectro expanded the design in 1956 with a six-string bass, rather like a guitar tuned one octave lower (or an electric bass with two extra treble strings, depending on how you look at it). The quality and design of the Danelectro models were not up to Fullerton standards, however, and when Fender brought out its own six-string bass (known simply as the Bass VI) in 1961, it seemed the design's moment of triumph had finally arrived.

Fender's designers returned to the elegant offset shape of the Jazzmaster (along with its vibrato), and installed three simple pickups with metal combs, controlled by switches on a plate (much like the Jaguar that would be released the following year). There was thus a panoply of sonic possibilities, but the Bass VI fell too much between two stools to appeal to the new generation of pop and blues guitarists. It was nonetheless used by the Beatles, the Cure, Glen Campbell and Aerosmith, and new musicians are rediscovering its underexplored charms.

Year of manufacture: 1963
Country: United States
Approximate resale value: £8,300
Hear it on: The Cure, 'Pictures of You' (1989)
Guitarist: Robert Smith

# Gibson
## ES-345

**Brands propose and guitarists dispose. Gibson has always tried to offer both more and less luxurious, high-end versions of the models in its range, often with considerable success. In the case of the ES-345, however, musicians have always preferred the most modest version.**

•

f price were not a consideration, few guitarists would choose an L-4 from the 930s over the far more eye-catching and sonically more crafted L-5. With the semi-hollow ES guitars from the end of the 1950s, however, the high-end models failed to follow up on the runaway success achieved by the first model the ES-335. This had been released in 1958, and two upgraded models (the ES-345 and the ES-355) followed in close succession.

All three are visually very similar, despite the differing degrees of decoration The ES-355 is at the top of the range, with a look derived from the Les Pau Custom (gold hardware, a bound headstock, a split diamond headstock ogo and block fret markers on an ebony fretboard). The ES-345 has the same headstock as the ES-335 but with no binding, although it does have double-parallelogram fret markers and gold hardware.

f these had been the only disparities, the three models would probably have been equally successful. The real difference that made guitarists avoid the 345 and 355 like the plague, however, was their electronics, which illustrated perfectly the adage that 'the perfect is the enemy of the good'. Not only was there a passive Varitone equalization circuit (which did indeed enable variation of the sound, but also absorbed some of the frequencies, though no one really knew how to use it anyway), but also – worst of all – these guitars were stereo (as the proud legend on the truss rod cover of this ES-345 proclaimed). A special cable was required to connect each pickup to a dedicated amplifier, and for most guitarists, this meant having to rewire the electronics to recapture the simplicity of the ES-335.

Despite this entirely reasonable drawback, these remained superb guitars, as is demonstrated by this model, on which the Custom Made plate hides pre-drilled holes to be used when the instrument is fitted with a Bigsby.

Year of manufacture: 1963
Country: United States
Approximate resale value: £16,700
Hear it on: Freddie King, 'Going Down' (1971)

CUSTOM MADE

# Martin
## OM-45 Deluxe

**Vintage Martins certainly have a knack for turning the heads of even the most avid collectors. Besides the standard models manufactured in the 1930s (which are already very expensive), however, there are some guitars of such rarity that these priceless treasures deserve the same status as a Stradivarius violin.**

•

The Martin range settled on shapes and model numbers in the 1930s that remain in use today, and it was from these that all the other brands drew inspiration for their own designs, in particular with the advent of neck joints at the fourteenth fret. This was also a time when the quality of the company's instruments was at its peak, despite the Great Depression, through the happy conjunction of a highly qualified factory workforce and the unparalleled quality of the wood that was available.

Such timber is no longer to be had, and Martin's luthiers now work at a radically different pace. Despite all the goodwill the brand has accumulated, it will never again scale the heights of its golden age, not least because the guitars in question have had almost a hundred years to age and improve – as long as they have been properly looked after.

Given its condition, this is undoubtedly the case for this OM-45 Deluxe. The OM (for Orchestra Model) shape was a way to have more bass than the brand's smaller models (0 and 00) while retaining the same shape as the 000, with a longer scale length to make the sound brighter. The quality achieved by the 45 range represents the epitome of construction in both the choice of woods and the decorative features, but there was a level of ornamentation even beyond this, indicated by the additional Deluxe designation. This featured additional inlays on the scratchplate, the sides of the bridge and even the bridge pins. No more than a dozen examples of this model were manufactured in 1930, making it one of the rarest (and most expensive) acoustic guitars in the world.

Year of manufacture: 1930
Country: United States
Approximate resale value: £834,100
Hear it on: Eric Clapton, 'Nobody Knows You When You're Down and Out' (*Unplugged*, 1992)

**Martin OM-45**
It is the distinctive floral mother-of-pearl inlay on the scratchplate that makes this OM-45 an OM-45 Deluxe, Martin's most luxurious model. There is, of course, also a discreet but superb snowflake on the bridge, and even the bridge pins have been given individual inlays.

# Gibson
## ES-295

**The solid-body electric guitar is associated with rock 'n' roll because of its omnipresence during the 1960s and 70s, but the pioneers of the genre were in fact mostly archtop fans. Scotty Moore, the most famous of them all, chose a model that was as flamboyant as the singer he accompanied, which is saying something.**

•

The heyday of Les Paul and Mary Ford (a married couple and also a double act on stage) was from the late 1940s to the beginning of the 50s. They were ubiquitous on the radio and also made television appearances (in black and white), so Gibson jumped at the chance of getting exposure for its instruments by endorsing Paul before it had even designed his signature model.

Paul was able to send requests to the workshop in Kalamazoo, and when he and Ford visited a hospital to play for the patients, one of them asked him for help ordering an ES-175 (a jazz archtop with a P90 pickup in the neck position) in a gold finish. The result was so beautiful that Gibson decided to make it a model in its own right, and the ES-295 was released in 1952, at the same time as the first iteration of the Les Paul.

The two guitars shared many features: a gold finish (although the back of the ES-295 was also painted gold, whereas the Les Paul was natural mahogany); cream-coloured P90 pickups; and a trapeze bridge, a system devised by Paul himself, which worked perfectly on the ES-295 but was less well adapted for use with the neck angle of the solid-body guitar.

In 1953 Moore, the guitarist of the Starlite Wranglers, traded in his Telecaster for a 1952 ES-295, and in 1954 he began to play with a young singer named Elvis Presley. He eventually swapped the guitar for a higher-end Gibson L-5, but the tracks he recorded for the Sun label in the meantime were so magical that the ES-295 will forever be associated with the first coming of the King.

Year of manufacture: 1954
Country: United States
Approximate resale value: £8,300
Hear it on: Elvis Presley, 'That's All Right' (1954)
Guitarist: Scotty Moore

FOR TOP PERFORMANCE OF YOUR NEW GIBSON
GIBSON POLISH
GIBSON STRINGS
INSTRUCTIONS
Gibson
GREATER TONAL RANGE
MORE BRILLIANT PERFORMANCE
LONGER SUSTAINING QUALITY
EASIER PLAYING ACTION

# Mosrite
## Joe Maphis Double Neck

**Mosrite guitars are among the most immediately identifiable designs of the 1960s, which is quite a statement, given the context. Of all the brand's output, however, there is no guitar that symbolizes the decade's kitschy, excessive side as perfectly as the double-neck Joe Maphis signature model.**

•

Semie Moseley began his career as an apprentice at Rickenbacker in 1952, and it was there that he met the German designer Roger Rossmeisl, from whom he learned a lot about what makes a guitar beautiful. He was also a friend of Paul Bigsby, an inventor who repaired motorbikes and made lap-steel guitars in his workshop, and it was Bigsby who encouraged Moseley to develop his ideas in his own space. Moseley produced his first guitars in his garage, most notably a double-neck for the country guitarist Joe Maphis, 'King of the Strings'.

In 1956 the Rev. Ray Boatright financed the creation of Moseley's brand, hence the Mosrite name, which combines the two surnames. The Moseley brothers got to work in their home town of Bakersfield, California, on a design that started out as the signature model for Maphis but would become the very essence of the brand. It boasted an asymmetrical shape with a longer horn on the treble side, an idiosyncratic vibrato design, in-house pickups and, most importantly, a stepped contour moulded into the top of the guitar, the famous 'German carve' borrowed from Rossmeisl.

Mosrite rose to prominence in 1963 thanks to a deal that put its guitars into the hands of the Ventures, stars of instrumental surf music and one of the era's most popular bands. The group's three guitarists swapped their Fenders for Mosrites and became an icon of the Bakersfield brand. Not long afterwards, Maphis designed a double-neck signature model with Mosrite. It is an eccentric instrument, but one that is easier to get at than his first double-neck, which, instead of the 12-string neck, had a 6-string neck tuned an octave higher. Although a designer of genius, Semie Moseley was unfortunately never a good businessman, and the brand's existence was always fraught with complication.

Year of manufacture: 1968
Country: United States
Approximate resale value: £4,200
Hear it on: Jimi Hendrix, 'Spanish Castle Magic' (1967)

# Gibson ES-250

**The end of the 1930s brought the start of electrification for Gibson guitars, and it was during this period of the instrument's prehistory that a very few musicians took up the invention and incorporated it into their musical vision. Charlie Christian is inseparable from this first era, and to some extent we are still living in the world he imagined.**

•

There are always earlier, smaller-scale experiments, but it was none other than Gibson that brought out the first true electric guitar model with the ES-150 (Electric Spanish) of 1936. This new designation, which is still in use in the brand's catalogue, was intended to differentiate the guitar from the lap-steels that were played flat across the knees and listed as EH (Electric Hawaiian) by the company. It should be noted that the fashion for Hawaiian music was in full swing, and at the time 'electric guitar' referred more often to a lap-steel than a so-called proper guitar. The 150 figure merely indicated the outlay of US$150 that was required to become the owner of such an instrument (and of the amplifier, also manufactured by Gibson, which was thrown in for the price).

The ES-150 was a sparsely decorated semi-hollow archtop guitar with a single pickup in the neck position. This pickup had a metal blade rather than the pole pieces that would later be adopted as standard for the P90. The pioneers who took up the ES-150 included Charlie Christian, a young virtuoso who was only 23 years old when he joined the clarinettist Benny Goodman's orchestra in 1939. He was the first to champion the guitar as a solo instrument in an orchestra – a feat that was made possible only by amplification – so we are all in his debt. Sadly, his career was extremely short: he was admitted to hospital with tuberculosis in 1941 and died of the disease the following year.

On occasion, Christian would also play the ES-250, Gibson's second electric model. As the name suggests, it was much more expensive, with far more ornate decoration. The pickup with which it was fitted was the same, however, and this type of pickup is to this day known as a Charlie Christian, to honour the first person to have wrung such an exciting sound from it.

Year of manufacture: 1939
Country: United States
Approximate resale value: £12,500
Hear it on: Benny Goodman, 'Breakfast Feud' (1941)
Guitarist: Charlie Christian

BASS
INSTRUMENT
VOLUME
TREBLE
BASS
NORMAL
VOLUME
TREBLE
-Amp
FENDER ELECT. INST. CO.
DESIGN & CIRCUITS
PATENTED
Fender

# Fender Troublemaker Telecaster Deluxe

**The 1970s was a decade of soul-searching for Fender, an era in which the single-coil pickups of the brand's lead models no longer seemed suited to a zeitgeist that demanded virtuoso solos doused in distortion and sustain. The brand would adapt in its own way, always retaining the character that had made it successful.**

•

The Les Paul was the big winner during the 1970s, even if most rock stars of the era played Bursts from the late 1950s rather than Gibson's contemporary output. In response to this competition, Fender hired the services of Seth Lover, the engineer who had designed the first humbucker for Gibson, and asked him for a Fender version of a twin-coil pickup. Thus the Wide Range was born. The new pickup put in its first appearance in 1972, in three new versions of the Telecaster: the Thinline (with two humbuckers), the Custom (with a humbucker in the neck position) and the Deluxe.

The last of these was a slightly odd creature, being equipped not only with two Wide Ranges but also with a large Stratocaster headstock. That made it the hybrid instrument of the range par excellence. With a belly cutaway at the back for comfort and a price of US$400, it was top of the range for the Teles of the era, and some even came fitted with a Strat vibrato. It failed to arouse much interest, however, and disappeared in 1981, until indie rock stars like Radiohead recognized its true worth, leading to a reissue in 2004.

Since such times, Chris Shiflett of the Foo Fighters has made it his signature model. The Deluxe design has also been used as a starting point for more daring experiments, such as this Troublemaker model, which was released in 2018 as part of the Parallel Universe range, Fender's attempt to subvert its own rules. With its mahogany neck and body, sunburst-finish maple cap, Tune-O-Matic-style bridge and cream-coloured plastic parts and binding, there is a strong nod to the Les Paul. If a Telecaster were crossed with a Burst, the result would undoubtedly be a Troublemaker.

Year of manufacture: 2018
Country: United States
Approximate resale value: £1,700
Hear it on: Foo Fighters, 'Bridge Burning' (2011)
Guitarist: Chris Shiflett

Fender
Fender
VOL
VOL
TONE
TONE

# Fender
# Whiteguard Telecaster

**The Telecaster is one of those eternal electric guitars, a model that has altered very little since its launch in the early 1950s and one on which you can always rely. Musicians and collectors nonetheless like to draw distinctions between the various different eras of what is truly a cult object, and this has given rise to the fascination with the whiteguard.**

•

'Whiteguard' is in fact an abbreviation of 'white pickguard', and it is a way of telling the difference between the first Telecasters (and the Broadcasters and Nocasters that preceded them), which had black Bakelite scratchplates, and those from the second era, with their white plastic guards. The change presumably came about to match the Tele guard to the scratchplate on the Stratocaster (the new addition to the Fender range), since whiteguard Teles are to be found from 1954 onwards. There was no wasting of materials in the Californian brand's factory, however, so blackguards and whiteguards coexisted until 1955.

There was also no thought at the time of presenting the whiteguard as a new model. The brand would chop and change its instruments without keeping musicians informed or allowing them a say in the colour or the particular features of a guitar (an option that is ultimately a rather recent luxury). The colour was changed to coincide with the switch to a white scratchplate, introducing a shade known as Blond that was in fact white with a hint of yellow, a much lighter hue than the Butterscotch of the first Teles. The finish would betray the life the guitar had lived; owned by heavy smokers, for example, it would turn a creamy yellow.

This superb example from 1956 clearly features two traces of wear beside the bridge, probably corresponding to where the musician rested his ring finger and pinky as he played.

Year of manufacture: 1956
Country: United States
Approximate resale value: £33,400
Hear it on: Merle Haggard, 'Working Man Blues' (1969)
Guitarist: Roy Nichols

VOX

# Kay
## Red Devil

**Of the American brands manufacturing cheap instruments in the 1960s, Kay stands out for its sheer scale. The Chicago company was a veritable empire and its catalogue included models that the passing of time has made more desirable than they were at the time, such as the K-592, nicknamed the 'Red Devil'.**

•

The Kay Musical Instrument Company opened its doors in 1931 and its Chicago factory produced guitars (not yet electric), lap-steels, double basses (including the one used by Bill Black for Elvis Presley's first recordings), violins and banjos. These instruments were manufactured both under the brand's own name and for others, in particular for mail-order catalogues, so you will also find Kay models branded as Montgomery Ward, Sears, Penncrest and Truetone. The company got up to speed very quickly when the electric revolution arrived, and was notably the second to sell an electric bass after the Fender Precision.

Kay went on to design a host of electrics models, including the Speed Demon series of quarter-body guitars, and strove to push its range upmarket in terms of finish and fittings. To polish its brand image, it even designed signature models for the jazz star Barney Kessel (who never played them, preferring his Gibson).

The Red Devil was launched in 1962 as part of the top end of the brand's range, costing US$200 at a time when a Gibson ES-335 would go for about $300. The beauty shown here looks fantastic, with a cap and back in superbly figured maple that is nicely set off by the transparent red finish. The twin pickups typical of the brand were nicknamed 'speed bumps' because of their shape, and the vibrato is based on a Bigsby.

The Red Devil may not have attained legendary status, but it remains a guitar with a very particular and inspiring sound. It is a sonic time machine that will take you back through the decades.

Year of manufacture: 1963
Country: United States
Approximate resale value: £800
Hear it on: Little Barrie, 'Why Don't You Do It' (2006)
Guitarist: Barrie Cadogan

NORMAL
VIBRATO
Fender
KAY
Fender
Fender
Bigsby
PATENT
NO.D-169,120

# Millimetric Instruments
## MGS2

**The prices of vintage instruments have risen to such giddy heights that it's tempting to say that they must come from an age when guitars were better. The market is driven largely by collectors, however, and today's luthiers do not lag behind the 1950s workforce at Fullerton and Kalamazoo in terms of sound and manufacturing quality; indeed, anything but.**

•

I would like to offer a purely personal opinion here: we are living in the golden age of the guitar. If your heart is set on an old-style Strat, you can have one made by the Fender Custom Shop, or buy a Squier and mod it with pickups that are easily acquired as aftermarket parts. If you desire something a little more off-the-wall, direct contact with artisans and designers around the world can be made with disconcerting ease online.

There have been original models with unique designs and small production runs in the past, of course: Travis Bean's Californian output from the 1970s, for example, with their aluminium necks and famed openwork headstock; or Teuffel from Germany, with its industrial, minimalist shapes of the 2000s. Back then, people had to go to trade shows or rely on their local clientele to spread the word, but this is no longer the case.

Millimetric Instruments is one of those courageous brands that are taking things to the next level. Its founder, Canadian Florian Bouyou, set up in business in 2012 after studying graphic communications and furniture design, and the MGS2, with its highly elegant, single-cutaway configuration, is his third design. The guitar is made entirely from black walnut, with a bolt-on neck that continues through the body to the bridge, and a headstock that is a clear tip of the hat to Bean. The bridge is an in-house creation, as are the pickups, which are reminiscent of a futuristic version of Danelectro's lipstick model.

The result will not be to everyone's taste, of course. Fans of this sort of thing know exactly where they can order one, and everyone else will just have to find what they are seeking elsewhere.

Year of manufacture: 2019
Country: Canada
Approximate resale value: £2,500
Hear it on: Alex Haines, Demo for James' Home of Tone (2021)

**Millimetric Instruments MGS2**

Unlike most luthiers, who order in their hardware and pickups from big suppliers of aftermarket parts, the Canadians at Millimetric Instruments do it all themselves, from this stainless-steel bridge with its brass saddles to the ultramodern control knobs and lipstick-style pickups.

# Esquire

**Nothing beats the Fender Esquire for simplicity, and alongside the crucial role it has played in guitar history, this model is also a symbol and a state of mind in itself. It is the guitar of choice for musicians who believe perfection is attained only when nothing more can be removed. Every single element of its design has a very good reason for being there, which means it has changed very little over the years.**

•

In the beginning was the Esquire. Long before such names as Broadcaster and Telecaster were being bandied about, Fender's first solid-body electric guitars were called the Esquire, and even the prototypes from 1949 featured only one pickup. The Esquire will always be the very first Fender, the guitar that opened the door for all the others. When the Telecaster achieved its great success, the Esquire would of course become its single-pickup variant, a kind of reverse take on history, as it were. It should be noted that the Esquire cost US$149.50 to the Telecaster's $189.50, a difference that was not big enough to justify going without the increased versatility offered by the neck pickup; this may explain the paucity of vintage Esquires around these days, compared to Telecasters.

The Esquire had a single pickup at the bridge, which at the time was almost unheard of, since guitarists' principal interest was in the round, full sound of the neck pickup. Country and rockabilly musicians, among them Luther Perkins (Johnny Cash) and Paul Burlison (Johnny Burnette), appreciated its brash and direct sound, however, followed a few years later by such idols as Syd Barrett (Pink Floyd) and Jeff Beck, whose Esquire (heavily sanded back to create comfort bevels similar to those on a Strat) made a whole generation of British Yardbirds fans yearn for a Fender.

A body, a neck, a pickup, a bridge and that's more or less it. The ingredients have not changed throughout the model's existence, and despite its removal from the catalogue in 1969, it has put in periodic reappearances that are fully appreciated by true connoisseurs. To need more than this is already to stray from the truth.

Year of manufacture: 1956
Country: United States
Approximate resale value: £20,900
Hear it on: Johnny Burnette & The Rock 'n' Roll Trio, 'Honey Hush' (1956)
Guitarist: Paul Burlison

FENDER
PAT. PEND

# Gibson
## 70s EDS-1275

**Gibson's famous double-neck is one of those instruments that fascinate guitarists, an object of such wild imagination that it demands attention. It has even become a symbol of the decadent pomp of 1970s rock. Originally, however, the model enjoyed only very limited success.**

•

The EDS-1275 model that Gibson released in the late 1950s was a hollow-body version very different from the modern notion of a double-neck guitar. It was not until 1963 that the 1275 became the 'double SG' by adopting the solid body, red coloration and general appearance of the era's star model. Musicians had no desire to cart around such an enormous instrument, however, and production ceased in 1968.

In 1971 'Stairway to Heaven' had just been recorded and Jimmy Page had to reproduce the 12-string parts and the 6-string solo on stage. The most viable solution was therefore a double-neck guitar. He put in a special order to Gibson and the irresistible rise of Led Zeppelin and the almost mythical status of that particular track did the rest.

Gibson re-released the EDS-1275 in 1974, in a minimally updated version with two screen-printed headstock logos (rather than inlays), 'witch hat' knobs and the slightly elongated headstocks typical of 1970s Gibsons. The available colours were also of their time, including Alpine White and Walnut, a light transparent brown that has since become a trademark of the single-neck SG.

The EDS-1275 would be spotted in the hands of Alex Lifeson (Rush) and Don Felder (Eagles), both of whom owned Alpine White versions, and its use was always justified by the need to reproduce several guitar overdubs in concert. Scott Holiday of the Rival Sons went for a Walnut finish for his (the one shown here). While there may be a good musical reason to use one of these instruments, we are too familiar with the flamboyant side of the average guitarist to say that it is not mostly about stage presence.

Year of manufacture: 1970s
Country: United States
Approximate resale value: £8,300
Hear it on: Rival Sons, 'Feral Roots' (2019)
Guitarist: Scott Holiday

# Gibson Explorer

**Some designs are just too far ahead of their time to find an audience, although the most beautiful eccentricities are sometimes vindicated with the passage of time. In the case of the Explorer, what started life as an oddity shunned by all has become one of the most sought-after guitars in the world.**

•

In 1957 Gibson president Ted McCarty saw that Fender was stealing his instruments' thunder and decided to bring out some models with shapes that were less traditional and more fun than usual. Things went a little too far in the other direction, however, and the three designs in question were too out there for their time. The range, named Modernistic, included the Flying V, the Explorer and the Modern(e). The last of these remained a prototype and never went into production, but the other two were manufactured in very small runs in the late 1950s: a total of 19 Explorers were made in 1958, and another 3 produced in 1959 before the model was officially discontinued (a few more examples with nickel hardware – no more than a dozen or so – were manufactured at the turn of the 1960s, however). These first models were called 'korina', the name dreamed up by Gibson for the exotic black limba wood used for the body, which was nicely accentuated by the guitars' natural finishes.

Several leading guitarists discovered the sonic and visual charms of the Explorer, in particular Eric Clapton (who trimmed back the bass side of his for easier playing), and Allen Collins of Lynyrd Skynyrd. Gibson restarted production in the mid-1970s, just as the Hamer brand was choosing the Explorer as the central model of its range, and numerous others would offer slightly adapted takes on the famous shape.

Since then, the extreme rarity of the originals has made them greatly sought-after (there are any number of fakes in circulation, of course). Even faithful replicas like this Murphy Lab guitar, which has a korina body and a Brazilian rosewood fretboard, sell for astronomical prices.

Year of manufacture: 2021
Country: United States
Approximate resale value:
for the replica shown here, £12,500;
for an original, £667,300
Hear it on: Lynyrd Skynyrd, 'Free Bird'
(*One More from the Road*, 1976)
Guitarist: Allen Collins

MESA
ENGINEERING

# Gretsch 6120
## Chet Atkins

**Observing the success of Gibson's Les Paul, the brand's competitor Gretsch was unable to stand by with arms folded, so its advertising managers set about finding the guitarist best suited to championing a signature model made in Brooklyn. Logically enough, it looked to Chet Atkins.**

•

When Gretsch offered Chet Atkins a partnership contract in 1955, it was truly picking the Nashville equivalent of Les Paul, since he was both a successful guitarist with his own instrumental albums and a famous producer (even producing Elvis Presley), not to mention an inveterate tinkerer and inventor. In response to Gibson's success with the Les Paul model in 1952, it was only logical for Gretsch to fight back with the 6120 Chet Atkins three years later.

The first version of the model was highly ornate, with tasteful Western detailing including a large G on the soundboard (as if branded with a hot iron), cow heads on the fretboard, cactuses and everything else besides. This country frippery was not at all to Atkins's taste (he had scarcely been consulted for his model) and they eventually disappeared, leaving just a single horseshoe on the headstock.

Gretsch listened to Atkins a lot more carefully over the choice of pickups. Essentially, the musician wished to eliminate background noise, and asked engineer Ray Butts to design a bespoke pickup. The upshot was the Filter'Tron (short for 'Filter electTronic noise'), Gretsch's humbucker, which came out more or less at the same time as Gibson's humbucker in 1957, in a fascinating moment of spontaneous parallel generation.

Leaving Atkins aside, the 6120 has become the Gretsch par excellence, an orange archtop perfect for country, rockabilly, punk and Americana. Many guitarists have adopted it, and it remains a sonic and visual benchmark.

Year of manufacture: 1961
Country: United States
Approximate resale value: £10,800
Hear it on: The Brian Setzer Orchestra, 'Sleepwalk' (1998)

Treble Booster
On/Off
Input
GUITAR SET
Strings
GRETSCH
BY
Bigsby
TOP OF THE POPS
BAND
HOSPITALITY
WORLD TOUR 2009
6/20 LON
BBC
TELEVISION
ARTIST

# ERIC CLAPTON

## THE MESSENGER

**Few musicians polarize guitarists as much as Eric Clapton. For some, the Brit is the ultimate bluesman, the man who brought a niche style to the general public, while for others he is a plunderer of Black American music who found success on the backs of the original artists. As is so often the case, the truth lies somewhere in between.**

•

Eric Clapton was born in Surrey, southern England, in 1945, just a few miles down the road from the childhood homes of Jeff Beck and Jimmy Page, two other giants of British blues whose destinies would forever be intertwined with his. After a complicated upbringing, he sought refuge in the guitar and discovered American music: the rock 'n' roll of the 1950s, then the blues of Robert Johnson, the Delta musician of the 1930s.

Clapton first joined the Yardbirds – a blues group bringing the songs of Muddy Waters to British adolescents – in 1963, before transferring in 1965 to John Mayall's Bluesbreakers. This was the line-up that created the legendary eponymous album on which Clapton unveiled to an incredulous world the overdrive achieved by plugging a Les Paul into a Marshall.

In 1966 he formed the power trio Cream with bassist Jack Bruce and drummer Ginger Baker, also virtuoso players, launching into extended solos in the middle of psychedelic adaptations of Delta blues classics. The battle of egos finally put paid to the band in 1968, and after stints with two short-lived groups (Blind Faith and Derek & the Dominos), Clapton went solo under his own name, releasing an eponymous debut album in 1970.

He brought out a slew of albums, achieving commercial success and introducing both the reggae of Bob Marley (with his cover of 'I Shot the Sheriff') and the folk of J J Cale (with his version of 'Cocaine') as he developed a Stratocaster sound that was bright, crunchy and unique. The 1980s were a little more complicated for Clapton, but he emerged more popular than ever after his stupendous *Unplugged* performance of 1992, a gig that single-handedly revived sales of acoustic guitars. Clapton has lived any number of musical lives since then, and only now, at almost 80, does he seem to be slowing his pace of production.

# Gibson
## J-200

**Whenever a highly ornate acoustic guitar model turns up from the pre-war period, you can bet your bottom dollar it's a commission from a singing cowboy. Their exploits may eventually have faded into obscurity, but these vigilantes of justice were true superstars in the 1930s and never passed up an opportunity to break into song, perched atop their faithful steeds.**

•

The advent of the J-200 was originally all about egos. Ray Whitley, a rising star of cowboy films in the 1930s, was not going to let Gene Autry and his magnificent Martin D-45 steal his thunder. Logically enough, Whitley sought out Gibson, Martin's main competitor, and helped to create an entirely new shape that would be the largest and most ornate ever to come out of the Kalamazoo factory.

The upshot was a jumbo guitar with a body as large as the imposing L-5 archtop, a nipped waist and mother-of-pearl inlays everywhere you looked, from the headstock to the bridge, not forgetting the fretboard. After producing this first example in 1937, Gibson decided to incorporate the model into the top of its range of acoustic flat tops at a price of US$200 (a Martin D-45 cost exactly the same at the time, and this was probably no coincidence). The new shape was dubbed the Super Jumbo and the guitar was rebadged as the SJ-200.

After the war the name was simplified to the J-200 and the guitar's construction in particular was crucially modified, with the body changing from rosewood to maple. This gave it a radically different sound from that of the Martin dreadnought, with a brighter, more penetrating character. It was this sound (along with its incredible appearance) that appealed to artists as varied as Elvis Presley, the Everly Brothers, George Harrison, Jimmy Page, Bob Dylan, Pete Townshend and Emmylou Harris, and the jumbo has lost none of its magnificence to this day.

Year of manufacture: 1959
Country: United States
Approximate resale value: £16,700
Hear it on: The Beatles, 'Here Comes the Sun' (1969)
Guitarist: George Harrison

# Fender
## Custom Telecaster

**Plain Janes can sometimes steal the show. The Telecaster may be the simplest guitar among Fender's great models, but it was the only one to be re-released in a truly higher-end version in the catalogues of the 1960s.**

•

Having good, better and best options is now a common marketing strategy and a perfectly standard way of organizing your catalogue, since offering three price points for three degrees of quality gives the consumer the illusion of choice. The current Fender catalogue even runs the risk of provoking the anxiety of choice; there are so many different iterations of each model, with more or less vintage or modern features and at prices ranging from modest to exorbitant for guitars that look incredibly similar.

The guitarists of the 1950s had the opposite problem: a single available version of the big models, with minimal options. You might be able to order your Strat as a hardtail (without a vibrato), but that was about it. In 1959, however, the Telecaster evolved into a more upscale incarnation, the Custom Telecaster. The principal difference was the arrival of cream-coloured double binding on the front and back of the body, a fancy touch made possible by the model's 'slab body' and that would have been impossible to incorporate into the chamfered body of the Stratocaster or Jazzmaster.

The other change was to the colour. At a time when all Telecasters were white and it was still impossible to order a custom colour, the Custom Telecaster came in three-tone sunburst, with red in addition to yellow and black. The marriage of a sunburst finish with binding has become iconic and can be seen in the hands of Bruce Springsteen and Andy Summers (the Police), for example.

In 1972 Fender accommodated a frequent request by replacing the Telecaster's neck pickup with a humbucker, and it was in such a configuration that the new Telecaster Custom made its first appearance, with a look (outsize scratchplate and four control knobs) that retained little from the first version shown opposite. Something may have been lost in translation, it must be said.

Year of manufacture: 1969
Country: United States
Approximate resale value: £10,000
Hear it on: The Police, 'Walking on the Moon' (1979)
Guitarist: Andy Summers

VOX
FENDER

# Gibson Super 400

**Gibson has existed as a brand since 1902, when Orville Gibson was making mandolins and related instruments in Kalamazoo, Michigan. The true birth of the Gibson company that made history dates to the 1920s, however, and the creation of the archtop guitar as we know it today.**

•

At the turn of the 20th century Orville Gibson hit upon the idea of applying the structural principles of mandolins and violins to the guitar, with a carved soundboard and a back that was thicker in the centre than at the sides. It was technically already an archtop, since the top was essentially curved. Still, the current design of this kind of instrument would not put in an appearance until 1922, when the Gibson company hired the luthier Lloyd Loar to revamp its range and he created the F5 and A5 mandolins, the H5 mandola, the K5 mandocello and the L-5 guitar, the model on which twin F-holes made their first appearance.

The L-5 established itself very quickly as the best guitar of the era and the only instrument capable of competing with the volume of banjos and mandolins in an orchestral setting. The competition began to take an interest in the archtop guitar market, however, in particular Epiphone from New York, which wasted no time in taking the fight to Gibson on its own territory. In 1931 Epiphone brought out the De Luxe, which was a little larger than the L-5, to which Gibson responded with the Advanced L-5 of 1935, whereupon Epiphone released the Super De Luxe. Gibson countered by making the Super 400 (its top-of-the-range model) even larger, and Epiphone's last word on the matter was the enormous Emperor.

The Super 400 was the last response from Gibson, which no doubt realized that this arms race was starting to bring diminishing returns. The model, which dates back to 1934, was a real work of art and represented an attempt on Gibson's part to distil all its visual and sonic expertise into a single guitar. Because of its prohibitive price of US$400 (nearly $10,000 today, and this was in the middle of the Great Depression!), few examples were manufactured (only 90 were made in 1935). Despite this lukewarm reception, however, its Art Deco lines proved a major influence on many other guitar-makers.

Year of manufacture: 1935
Country: United States
Approximate resale value: £12,500
Hear it on: Elvis Costello & The Imposters, 'Monkey to Man' (2004)

35 Gibson S400

# Silvertone
## Danelectro U1

**Guitars for beginners are now manufactured in China and Indonesia as a matter of course. In the 1950s there was no question of sending instruments to the other end of the world to take advantage of lower-priced labour, so other means of providing cheap guitars made in the United States had to be found.**

•

Nathan Daniel rarely gets a mention when the history of the electric guitar is discussed, although his role in developing new instruments that shaped the popular music of the 20th century was not so different from that of Leo Fender or George Beauchamp. A New Yorker of Lithuanian extraction, he began to design amplifiers before World War II before setting up his Danelectro brand in 1946.

It was under this name that Daniel opened the world's first amplifier factory, a bold step justified by the huge orders he was receiving from his two main customers, Montgomery Ward and Sears, Roebuck & Co. Both were department-store chains that also maintained extensive mail-order catalogues, and it was to their models (Airline in the case of Montgomery, Silvertone for Sears) that beginner guitarists would turn every Christmas. Danelectro manufactured for both while also retaining its own brand for independent music shops. Its amplifiers blazed a trail for other brands at the time by being among the first to incorporate such unheard-of options as built-in tremolo or reverb.

Danelectro entered the guitar market in 1954, faced with the challenge of manufacturing cheap but reliable solid-body instruments, and Daniel hit upon the idea of assembling a poplar frame with a front and back made of hardboard (sheets of glued wood fibres known as Masonite in America) with vinyl-covered sides – all cheap materials for a guitar that would be easy to manufacture in large runs. For his pickups, he created the famous 'lipstick' model in its metal tube, which boasted a unique look and sound, and it is precisely this unique sonic palette that has ensured Danelectro's lasting popularity.

Year of manufacture: 1959
Country: United States
Approximate resale value: £800
Hear it on: Led Zeppelin, 'Kashmir' (1975)
Guitarist: Jimmy Page

Gibson's double-neck was also available in a version called the
12-string neck replaced by a mandolin neck. This had originally
affair but evolved into the more traditional 8-string format wit
string courses. Lastly, the EDS-1275 marked the first appearance
successful body shape featuring two pointed horns that was to b

Year of manufacture: 1959
Country: United States
Approximate resale value: £12,500
Hear it on: The Band, 'The Weight'
(*The Last Waltz*, 1978)
Guitarist: Robbie Robertson

Gibson
Gibson

# D'Angelico
## New Yorker

**The jazz archtop was the guitar to beat in the 1930s. While such top-shelf brands as Gibson and Epiphone fought relentlessly to curry favour with professional players, genuine connoisseurs were in fact turning to the work of John D'Angelico, a true artist in the field.**

•

D'Angelico was born in the Little Italy district of Manhattan, New York, in 1905. As his name might suggest, his family was of Italian origin, and it was from his great-uncle that he learned how to make violins and mandolins, two instruments from which he adopted the principles that underlay his archtop guitars. In 1932, shunning the idea of a large workshop, he set up the D'Angelico Guitars studio and worked with one or two apprentices to guarantee the excellence of the 35 instruments he made each year. Inspired from the outset by Gibson's L-5, he developed his own designs, of which the most renowned is still the famous New Yorker, which pays homage to Manhattan's Art Deco buildings.

Jimmy D'Aquisto became D'Angelico's apprentice in 1952 at the age of only 17. He proved a valuable collaborator and the two worked together to refine D'Angelico's designs from the late 1950s, a period that is generally considered the peak of the luthier's output. These featured sunburst finishes, and stranger shapes and more sophisticated decoration than their forerunners.

After D'Angelico's death in 1964, D'Aquisto manufactured guitars under his own name until 1995, taking up the baton of the beautiful archtops from New York without ever becoming subservient to the designs of the past. D'Aquisto and D'Angelico are considered the two greatest archtop luthiers in history, and their creations are worthy of display in any museum. They were honoured in 2011 with an exhibition at the prestigious Metropolitan Museum of Art in New York, entitled *Guitar Heroes: Legendary Craftsmen from Italy to New York*. No more than 1,164 guitars would bear the name of D'Angelico between 1932 and 1964, making them particularly prized by fans of outsize archtops.

Year of manufacture: 1960
Country: United States
Approximate resale value: £50,000
Hear it on: Johnny Smith, 'Walk, Don't Run' (1964)

Fender Bassman
Marshall
INPUTS
NORMAL
VOLUME
TREBLE
BASS
VIBRATO
VOLUME
TREBLE
BASS
REVERB
SPEED
INTENSITY
Deluxe Reverb-Amp
FENDER ELECT. INST. CO.

# AMPLIFIERS

## AT THE OTHER END OF THE GUITAR LEAD

**This book has introduced you to many historic guitars, but for electric playing, the instrument itself is only half the story. At the other end of the lead you will find an amplifier. Unlike the guitar models, which have stayed relatively unchanged since the 1960s, the world of amplification is in a state of constant flux that continues to this day.**

•

It all started in the 1930s. Some kind of amplifier had to be devised as the electrified guitar was invented, and amplifiers very similar to the radios of the time were initially used to connect lap-steels and Gibson ES-150s. These were valve circuits of limited power, and as soon as the volume was pushed a little too much, the result was simultaneously distortion and feedback.

The arrival of the vanguard of solid-body guitars in the 1950s was accompanied by the first real range of professional amplifiers, which included models that have remained a benchmark to this day (such as the Fender 'tweed' amps, so called because of their cloth covering). Leo Fender developed an entire range, from the tiny Champ to the outsize Twin, with every size in between to suit all circumstances. Tweeds tended to overdrive quite quickly, and Fender refined its circuits to create the 'blackface' version of its models in 1964. Many of these came fitted with reverb and a tremolo channel, but, above all, they were amplifiers that would remain clean for much longer. This striving for clean amplification would drive the change-over to the transistor amplifiers that, with rare exceptions, have become the preserve of beginners.

At this time Jim Marshall, a UK shop owner with an understanding of the genius of the tweed Fender Bassman, copied it with British parts, and the first Marshall was born. In response to a request from Pete Townshend (the Who) in 1965, he created the Marshall stack (an amplifier head and two separate speaker cabinets), which remains the ultimate symbol of rock guitar. Where Fender had sought to avoid distortion, Marshall understood that it was a major selling point.

From this point on, manufacturers sought to push the gain stage ever further, by modifying either Fenders (Dumble and Mesa/Boogie) or Marshalls (Soldano and Friedman). Mass-produced amplifiers now rub shoulders with exclusive boutique models, and have been joined by simulators, digital reproductions of historic amplifiers that make life easier for musicians who have no roadies to take the strain.

# Taylor
# GT K21e

**The travel guitar is a market in its own right, and most brands have taken an interest at various times. Taylor has really made the sector its own, however, producing first the Baby, then the GS Mini. With this extremely well-appointed GT, the Californian brand has elevated the mini guitar to a work of art.**

•

The search for the origins of the modern travel guitar leads back to the end of the 19th century, when Martin brought out its '5' shape with the 5-18 and the 5-15. This ultra-compact format was chosen by Sting for his signature model with the Nazareth brand, and it has been nicknamed the 'terz guitar' because it is generally tuned a minor third higher than standard to compensate for its shorter scale length.

Things have moved on since then, and the mini guitar has become both a travel requisite and a serious instrument for the stage and the studio. There was the Martin Backpacker of 1991, with its strange, stripped-down shape, then the Baby Taylor of 1996, which made a significant contribution to the success of the Californian brand and has been spotted in the hands of Damon Albarn (Blur) and Taylor Swift. Martin countered with the Little Martin (2003), which became the instrument of choice for Ed Sheeran and others, but Taylor had the last word with the GS Mini (2011), a perfect blend of compact size and massive sound.

The GT (Grand Theater) shape, launched in 2021, sits between the slightly larger Grand Concert and the more compact GS Mini. It represents an intriguing twist, being a mini shape that ultimately inspired an entire range of 'normal'-sized guitars. Apart from its ebony fretboard, this Taylor GT K21e is made of koa throughout, a wood native to Hawaii that is particularly prized for its spectacular appearance. It's a great way to showcase a shape that was originally just an easy way to fit a guitar into a car boot.

Year of manufacture: 2021
Country: United States
Approximate resale value: £2,500
Hear it on: Gorillaz, 'Feel Good Inc.' (2005)
Guitarist: Damon Albarn

Taylor

# Gibson
## SG Custom

**The entire range followed suit with a cosmetic update when Gibson changed the shape of the Les Paul in 1961, and this presented an opportunity to revisit some of the colour options and hardware choices. The SG Custom naturally found its way to the top of the range, and this example has been played by some famous fingers.**

•

Gibson completely redesigned the shape of its Les Paul models in 1961 with a view to reviving sales, introducing double Florentine cutaways, a chamfered mahogany body (with no maple cap) and an ultra-thin, slim-taper neck. At the top of the range, the Les Paul Custom turned from black to white but retained its ebony fretboard (with block fret markers), bound headstock, split diamond logo and gold hardware. It was also the most heavily loaded model both electronically and mechanically, with three humbucking pickups (which would normally have had gold covers, although they have been removed from this example) and an idiosyncratic vibrato with a folding arm that moved laterally, hence the name Sideways Vibrola.

From 1961 onwards this was the model of choice for Mary Ford, who sang in a duo she had formed with her husband, Les Paul. Notably, this instrument features on the cover of the album *Warm and Wonderful* from 1962 (on which we can also tell from his guitar's headstock that Paul had instead opted for the Standard version). The guitar disappeared into obscurity when Ford retired from show business, until an episode of the reality television show *Pawn Stars* in 2012, in which Ford's nephew sold the very same Les Paul Custom to a pawn shop in Las Vegas. This beautiful white guitar eventually resurfaced on Facebook Marketplace in 2023 and was bought by Gibson for its archive.

Year of manufacture: 1961
Country: United States
Approximate resale value:
for this example, which belonged to Mary Ford, approx. £125,100;
for the same model with no provenance, £25,000
Hear it on: Sister Rosetta Tharpe, 'Up above My Head'
(live on the 1960s TV show *Gospel Time*)

VARI-HANDLE
Les Paul
CUSTOM

# Epiphone
## E422T

**Epiphone is now well known as a sub-brand of Gibson and a name that allows the Nashville empire to bring out instruments of Chinese manufacture without compromising its brand image. There was a time, however, when Epiphone was an independent producer, a major player in the first era of the electric guitar and even a serious competitor to Gibson.**

•

The story of Epiphone begins in the Ottoman Empire – in Smyrna (now İzmir, Turkey) in 1873, when the Greek instrument-maker Anastasios Stathopoulos set up a factory. Having moved to New York in 1908, he died in 1915, whereupon his son Epaminondas took over the family business, dreaming up the name Epiphone – derived from his nickname, 'Epi' – in 1928. This was also the year in which the first guitars left the company's workshops in Queens, Epiphone's output having previously been restricted to mandolins and banjos.

The fashion of the day was for archtops, so Epiphone found itself in direct competition with Gibson, offering similar-looking guitars that were bigger or more ornate, with the famous New Yorker pickups that had a rounder, fuller sound than Kalamazoo's P90s. The two brands even ended up tearing strips off each other in their marketing when Epiphone responded to the advertising slogan 'Only a Gibson is good enough' with a scathing campaign headed 'When "good enough" isn't good enough'. Brutal.

Epiphone had also teamed up with Les Paul for his electronics research, allowing the guitarist to use its manufacturing equipment on Sundays, when the staff were not at work. The necks for the various 'Logs' (his experimental solid-bodies) were Epiphones, and when he became a Gibson artist, Paul continued to play them, simply changing the headstock logo.

This E422T is a neat example of the simple yet effective models manufactured by Epiphone in New York. It is a semi-hollow archtop with minimal decoration, but the few ornamental details (white knobs, New Yorker pickups, scratchplate featuring the brand's 'E') ensure that it is immediately identifiable.

Year of manufacture: 1951
Country: United States
Approximate resale value: £2,500
Hear it on: Gillian Welch, 'The Way It Goes' (2011)
Guitarist: Dave Rawlings

# Gibson
# HG Century of Progress

**Some guitars have become legendary for their sound or the musicians who played them, and some simply have such a striking, immediately identifiable appearance that they are impossible to miss. It shouldn't be difficult to guess the category into which the Gibson Century of Progress falls.**

•

The Chicago World's Fair of 1933 celebrated the city's 100th anniversary, spreading some vitally needed optimism during the Great Depression with the motto 'A Century of Progress'. Almost 50 million visitors came to admire the various pavilions, and this enthusiasm did not escape Gibson's attention. The firm accordingly decided to commemorate the event.

Gibson selected the L-00, a recent model, as the starting point for the design of the L-C (C for Century of Progress). This compact-format guitar had been released in 1931, but for the new model the mahogany of the body was replaced with highly figured maple, which looked more luxurious. Perhaps most notably, the fretboard and headstock were covered with pearloid, a fancy kind of plastic often found on the accordions and radio sets of the time. The headstock logo and fret markers were cut out and recycled from banjo fretboards left over at the factory, giving the whole thing a look that was immediately identifiable.

This particular example is the HG (Hawaiian Guitar) model, as can be seen from the neck joint at the twelfth fret. The design of this version of the L-C was intended to allow slide playing, with the guitar laid flat across the knees.

The Gibson L-C was produced only between 1933 and 1939, and very few examples are still in existence. A batch of about a hundred was reissued in 1994, and this became the inspiration for British singer Elvis Costello's signature model of 2008. No reissue has yet been made of the guitar in the HG Century's 12-fret format, however, and it remains a beautiful oddity that is typical of its time.

Year of manufacture: 1936
Country: United States
Approximate resale value: £5,800
Hear it on: Elvis Costello, 'Jimmie Standing in the Rain' (2010)

# Fender
## Acoustasonic Jazzmaster

**Contrary to what might be feared (given the countless reissues and copies of vintage guitars), the development of the instrument did not suddenly cease in 1968. Many brands have continued to explore new designs and more or less viable ideas, sometimes achieving real success, as is the case with Fender's Acoustasonic range.**

•

Necessity is said to be the mother of invention, and it is clearly the case with guitars that innovations often seem to offer solutions to the problems musicians encounter in their daily lives as artists. How can you play an acoustic guitar on stage without immediately descending into feedback, but without sacrificing the open resonance of the instrument? How can you move from acoustic to electric in the same song without including a break?

Several hybrids somewhere between an electric and an electro-acoustic have been attempted in response to such burning questions, including the first Acoustasonic of 2010, which blended a piezo transducer and a classic pickup neck on a modest electric Tele. The results were not entirely satisfactory, however, and Fender turned to two specialists in the field to work on a complete revision of the design. These were Tim Shaw, the 'pickup guru' who had designed pickups for Gibson in the 1980s, and Larry Fishman, the global specialist in amplification systems for acoustic guitars.

The upshot was the Acoustasonic Telecaster, which was released in 2019. Purists were immediately outraged, but such musicians as Jack White, Olivia Jean and J Mascis seized upon the new instrument to make music on stage. The new Acoustasonic was a mini acoustic shaped like a slightly deeper Telecaster, with construction and bracing specially designed to optimize output despite its reduced dimensions, and a bridge pickup developed specifically for the model. The Fishman preamp did the rest to perfect its acoustic voicings. The design was so successful that there are now versions shaped like Fender's two other stars, the Stratocaster and the Jazzmaster, the latter of which we see here in a very beautiful Ocean Turquoise.

Year of manufacture: 2022
Country: United States
Approximate resale value: £1,100
Hear it on: The Raconteurs, 'Only Child'
(2019, in concert)
Guitarist: Jack White

MAKO SERIES

# Guild
# S-200 Thunderbird

**Despite its chaotic history, which has made the various models rather difficult to keep track of, the Guild brand designed acoustic and electric guitars that have contributed to the sounds of great artists and continue to fascinate to this day. Of its classic designs, the S-200 Thunderbird is undoubtedly the most striking and audacious.**

•

Guild dates back to 1952, when the jazz guitarist Alfred Dronge was running a music shop in New York City. Both ventures meant that he was good friends with the workers at Epiphone, a brand that would eventually move to Philadelphia as a way of breaking the strikes being held in New York. As a result, numerous skilled luthiers found themselves out of work, and Dronge took advantage of this to hire them and establish a new brand for New York: Guild.

Since Dronge was a jazz musician and Epiphone had specialized in this field, the first Guild models were mainly archtops, but it began very quickly to produce flat tops (steel-strung acoustics) as well, followed by a solid-body range in 1963, just before the British Invasion swept America and made electrics fashionable. This last range included the sensible-looking Jetstar; the Polara, which resembled an offset SG (and was the guitar of choice for Kim Thayil of Soundgarden a quarter of a century later); and the top-of-the-range Thunderbird.

The last of these took its name from a convertible model made by Ford and sported a design that was particularly daring for the time. In addition to its elongated, offset shape, its twin humbuckers, its Hagström vibrato and a welter of knobs and switches, the Thunderbird boasted a secret feature: a folding stand built into the back of the guitar. This was in fact simply a metal rod that could be deployed at an angle of 45 degrees to the rear of the instrument, and it is unlikely to have been this 'improvement' that made the Thunderbird appeal to such musicians as Muddy Waters and Dan Auerbach (the Black Keys).

Year of manufacture: 1960s
Country: United States
Approximate resale value: £5,800
Hear it on: Muddy Waters, 'I Just Want to Make Love to You' (*Electric Mud*, 1968)

**Guild S-200 Thunderbird**
The Thunderbird came out in 1963, a year after the Fender Jaguar. In addition to the automotive inspiration of the two names, there is a sense that Guild wished to compete with the Californian giant by including so many switches on its top-of-the-range model. These three small selectors have their own scratchplate, and there is another chromed plate with an additional switch.

# Fender
## Broadcaster

**If you were forced to identify a precise starting point for the solid-body electric guitar, the market launch of the Fender Broadcaster in 1950 would be a fairly logical choice. This, the original model, has lost none of its relevance many decades later.**

•

Leo Fender was originally a repairman for radios and sound equipment in Fullerton, just south of Los Angeles, and went on to design his own amplifiers. He first took an interest in the lap-steel guitar, an instrument of Hawaiian origin much in fashion during the 1940s and made from a solid block of wood (or plastic) so that it would not feed back when amplified.

Fender applied this principle to the guitar, inventing an instrument of great simplicity whose manufacture could be systematized to the nth degree. There was a bolt-on maple neck with an integrated fretboard, an entirely unchamfered body made from a single block of wood, a metal bridge directly containing the treble pickup, and that was about all. The instrument was so basic compared to the beautiful archtops made by other brands that it attracted ridicule when it was launched in 1950. The competition was yet to realize that Fender had just blazed a trail for the instrument's future.

To emphasize the futuristic aspects of his invention, Fender christened it the Broadcaster in reference to the radio, a medium that was all the rage at the time. Sadly, Gretsch, which already had a drum kit called the Broadkaster, sent Fender a cease-and-desist letter demanding that the brand change the name of its new instrument. Fender was taken by surprise and had no choice but to put out Broadcasters with no model name on their headstocks for a few months in 1951; logically enough, collectors call these extremely rare guitars 'No-casters'.

Year of manufacture: 1950
Country: United States
Approximate resale value: £66,700
Hear it on: Tom Petty and the Heartbreakers, 'Breakdown' (1976)
Guitarist: Mike Campbell

FENDER
FULLERTON, CALIFORNIA

# Fender
# 1957 blond Stratocaster

**It did not take long for the Stratocaster to become an icon readily adopted by the discerning guitarist of the mid-1950s, and Fender has since made choices that allow it to offer the best variants of this new instrument without compromising its conveyor-belt production.**

•

Back when musicians would go directly to a luthier when they wanted to have a bespoke instrument made, it was standard practice to specify exactly what was required. With the arrival of the industrial model of production and its application to the guitar by Fender in 1950, however, the question arose of how the big brands' guitars might be adapted to an individual's particular needs. There were, of course, tinkerers who could take matters into their own hands – such as Les Paul, who routinely modified the Gibsons that bore his name – but for others the options were limited.

At Fender, the official catalogue did not allow a custom colour to be selected until the turn of the 1960s, and before that you had to be an artist of sufficient importance or good fortune to put in a special order at the Fullerton factory. The standard-issue Stratocaster came in a sunburst of two colours (black and yellow) in the 1950s, then of three (with the addition of red) in the 1960s. Any other colour was thus a special order, or a flight of fancy by Fender for some reason or other.

There was one exception to this rule, however. The finish known as White Blond (a transparent white) that was standard on the Telecaster in the second half of the 1950s was also available on the Strats of this period for a supplementary fee, and the combination of a blond finish with gold hardware was known as the Mary Kaye Strat, after a singer of Hawaiian music whose photos with that instrument had become hugely famous. It was also possible to order a sunburst Strat with no vibrato (called a hardtail) for a lower price, so there were officially three versions in the catalogue.

The guitar shown opposite is a blond (without gold hardware) belonging to Joe Bonamassa. It's all the more rare for being in superb condition, right down to the 'ashtray' tremolo cover, which has not been lost.

Year of manufacture: 1957
Country: United States
Approximate resale value: £58,400
Hear it on: Jimmie Vaughan, 'Just a Game' (2019)

VOLUME
TONE
TONE

# Gibson
# Custom Shop 1959 Les Paul Standard

**Gibson took its time, but it got there. Ever since guitarists started asking for another Les Paul like the Burst, the brand has constantly striven to get close to it, with greater or lesser success. The artificial ageing techniques, known as relicing, that are now in use almost make it more of a replica than a reissue.**

•

When Eric Clapton and Mike Bloomfield picked up sunburst Les Pauls at the very end of the 1950s (from 1958 to 1960), guitarists began to ask Gibson to re-release the model, since production had been halted. Les Paul was brought back on board, and in 1968 the brand re-released the Gold Top and the Custom – everything except what the public actually wanted. There followed a few isolated initiatives from shops that placed special orders, but there would be no real attempt at producing a Burst before the Heritage model of 1980.

Gibson has continued to perfect the art of reissuing with increasingly impressive results. Others have addressed the area, in particularluthiers who have made very plausible reproductions, such as Max Baranet and Kris Derrig. Ironically enough, it was a reproduction made by Derrig that Slash played on the first Guns N' Roses album, sending sales of actual Gibson Les Pauls into the stratosphere.

Gibson opened its Custom Shop in 1986 to concentrate on instruments at the very top of the range, and the luthier Tom Murphy began to develop his artificial ageing techniques. He is currently head of the Murphy Lab, the Custom Shop department devoted to relicing.

The reissue that is in the greatest demand is still the Les Paul Standard of 1959, with its big frets and perfect neck. This Cherry Tea Burst is a model that was specially released to celebrate the sixtieth anniversary of the original.

Year of manufacture: 2019
Country: United States
Approximate resale value: £6,700
Hear it on: Guns N' Roses, 'Welcome to the Jungle' (1987)
Guitarist: Slash

# Gibson L-00

**Gibson was not entirely unsympathetic to the financial difficulties musicians faced during the Great Depression, and although the Kalamazoo brand maintained a high-end image, it was able to offer instruments at reasonable cost without sacrificing the quality that had cemented its reputation.**

•

An unprecedented crisis dealt the American population a resounding blow in the 1930s. The stock market collapse of 1929 had already devastated the country's economy, but dust storms in the Southern states (which came to be known as the Dust Bowl) in the years that followed were the final straw for such regions as Oklahoma and Texas, and millions of workers left to seek a better life as far afield as California.

Musicians were equally affected. Few could afford the luxury instruments sold by Martin and Gibson, the industry's gold standards, so they had to fall back on Washburns or Stellas, guitars that lacked the reputation for quality but did not sell for the same price either.

To staunch this haemorrhage of customers, the big brands elected to stock less sophisticated guitars as well so that they could compete on an (almost) level playing field. Gibson, whose focus had previously been much more on archtops than flat tops, brought out the L-00 in 1931. This compact model was made entirely from mahogany (apart from its rosewood fretboard, of course), and its aesthetic adornments had been stripped back to the absolute minimum. At the time of its release, it was available only in black, a very practical choice for masking a wood that did not always look perfect. A sunburst finish would become standard by the middle of the decade.

The L-00 is a vintage model currently much in favour with musicians, since its mahogany gives it a very soft, warm tone (not necessarily Gibson's intention) and the manufacturing quality was up to Kalamazoo factory standards despite its reduced price. The association of these 'little' Gibsons with the Delta bluesmen, in particular because of the famous photo of Robert Johnson with an L-1 (which was probably not his), has only augmented their undeniably romantic allure.

Year of manufacture: 1930s
Country: United States
Approximate resale value: £4,200
Hear it on: Robert Johnson, 'Ramblin' on My Mind' (1936)

# Gibson
## 1957 Les Paul

**The fascination of some experts for a specific guitar model from a particular year might seem pointless and ridiculous from the outside, but a closer look at the evolution of great instruments shows that a few months can change everything in terms of historical importance, sound and vintage status.**

•

The 1957 Gibson Les Paul is one of those instruments that existed for only a few months, yet left an indelible mark on the world of guitars. It was during this year that Gibson launched the humbucker, its new pickup model. Up to this point, there had been only the P90, which came out in 1946, and this single-coil pickup was beset with problems in that it picked up extraneous noise very easily. Ted McCarty entrusted the engineer Seth Lover with the task of designing a pickup that would combat mains hum, giving rise to the name 'humbucker'. This new pickup featured twin coils, and it transpired that not only was it far more resistant to noise, but also it had a rounder, creamier sound and a higher output that would prove just the ticket when the guitarists of the 1960s began their search for the ultimate overdriven sound, even if that was far from the original goal.

By this time, Gibson had filed a patent application for its pickup, which is why a 'Patent Applied For' sticker is often to be found on the underside of these first humbuckers. That has given rise to their nickname 'PAF', initials capable of inspiring the imagination of any guitarist.

Within the Les Paul range, the PAF was installed on both the Custom and the Standard, which at the time was called the Les Paul Model. It was this famous guitar with its Gold Top finish that would change to Cherry Sunburst in the summer of 1958 (so the Gold Top/humbucker configuration lasted scarcely a year). This version with black plastic pickup rings (rather than cream) was available for a far shorter period of only a month. Such differences cost collectors a pretty penny.

Year of manufacture: 1957
Country: United States
Approximate resale value: £100,100
Hear it on: The Allman Brothers Band, 'In Memory of Elizabeth Reed' (1971)
Guitarists: Duane Allman, Dickey Betts

Fender Bandmaster

# Rickenbacker
## Combo 400

**Rickenbacker is generally considered the brand of the Beatles and the 12-string electric guitar. Although there is nothing to be ashamed of there (anything but!), it was also a pioneer playing an absolutely crucial role in the quest to create the modern electric guitar. And somewhere along the way, there was the Combo.**

•

Adolph Rickenbacher Americanized his surname when he joined George Beauchamp (who already had the first resonator guitars to his name) in setting up the Rickenbacker brand in California in 1931. These two pioneers worked together to design the 'frying pan' lap-steel with its 'horseshoe' pickup, the first solid-body guitar, and this was to have a major influence on all subsequent attempts at electrification.

In addition to their lap-steels, which were played flat across the knees, they also had an interest in the 'Spanish' guitar market, in particular with their Electro-Spanish Ken Roberts of 1935. Released a year before Gibson's ES-125, it was the first electric guitar on the market, not to mention the first signature electric guitar in history and the first to feature a vibrato (the Vibrola that Les Paul would fit on all his Gibsons in the 1950s).

The truly original design for a solid-body electric Rickenbacker dates back to 1956, however, and the advent of the Combo 400. Here we note a tulip shape with two cutaways that make the model immediately recognizable (as well as allowing easier access to the treble side), along with a body mostly covered by an anodized gold scratchplate, guaranteeing easy visibility on a floodlit stage. Most importantly, it had a through neck, a structural choice that would become a Rickenbacker staple, achieved by extending the neck to form the central part of the body, with a wing attached to either side – the secret to improved resonance.

The Combo 450 with a second pickup would follow, but the 400 had only a small neck pickup. An exception is this example once belonging to Rory Gallagher, who installed a bridge pickup; judging by the other holes in the scratchplate, it was probably not the first modification.

Year of manufacture: 1957
Country: United States
Approximate resale value: £4,200
Hear it on: Cheap Trick, 'Dream Police' (1979)
Rhythm guitarist: Robin Zander

FUZZ
VOLUME
WARNING
STOP
REVERSE
DITTO
tc electronic
BOOST
DRY
WET
Mosquite Blender
ONE CONTROL
Dan Drive
SECRET WEAPON
SAT
VOL

# EFFECTS

## MAKING A LITTLE DIFFERENCE

**In the beginning was the Guitar. Then it was amplified, and then guitarists saw that they could modify the noise made by these two elements by inserting little boxes between the two. Since then, effects have become an essential component of the sound of any self-respecting guitarist, to the extent that some have made them the linchpin of their style. But it all started by accident.**

•

In 1961 the country singer Marty Robbins was recording his song 'Don't Worry', but he had encountered a problem: the channel on the mixing desk into which the group's baritone guitarist was plugged was faulty, resulting in a scratchy, fuzzy tone. However, Robbins was inspired to keep the take as it was, and the song attracted attention for this particular sound. Musicians who subsequently came specially to that studio to get the same effect were most disappointed to learn that the mixing desk had been repaired, so the engineer Glenn Snoddy designed a box that could be plugged in between the bass (or guitar) and the amplifier to re-create this 'faulty' effect. Gibson released the circuit under its Maestro brand to create the first fuzzbox in history, which was to find its place in legend on the Rolling Stones' '(I Can't Get No) Satisfaction' of 1965. The British went on to make a copy, calling it the Tone Bender and the Fuzz Face, in one of those odd cases where the replica outdoes its original inspiration.

Effects had already been incorporated into some amplifiers or produced in the form of large external cabinets (reverb tanks, tremolo and tape echo), but from 1966 onwards, effects pedals flourished and multiplied. They became an essential element of the 1970s via such American brands as Electro-Harmonix and MXR, followed by Boss and Ibanez from Japan. In addition to fuzz, overdrive (which reproduced amplifier distortion) and modulation effects would soon appear.

The advent of digital technology in the 1980s resulted in pedals that were capable of producing reverb and delay effects, and modern units with a footprint the size of a cigarette packet can now emulate an entire sound chain. Most guitarists are also still fascinated with the little sonic boxes that they link together on pedalboards of more or less gigantic size.

# Gibson
## ES-175

**It is impossible for one guitar to be ideal for every context. The secret of the ES-175's long-term success, however, is that Gibson properly understood the advantages of an instrument made from less refined timber than its big archtops, a guitar specifically designed to be amplified without needing the flattering volume of its hollow body.**

•

The ES-175 is one of the longest-lived models in the Gibson catalogue, having been released in 1949 and still available in some form or another to this day (despite being officially deleted from the catalogue in 2019). Even the Les Paul did not enjoy such continuous popularity, since it was discontinued between 1961 and 1968.

The explanation for this success is simple enough: the ES-175 is a highly versatile instrument that has proved perfect in any number of contexts. It is the instrument of choice for blueswoman Bonnie Raitt, jazzers Pat Metheny, Jim Hall, Joe Pass and Herb Ellis, and rockers Steve Howe (Yes) and Buck Dharma (Blue Öyster Cult).

At first sight, you might mistake it for a traditional jazz archtop, but the ES-175 is made from laminated wood (thin strips glued together) rather than solid timber. The archtops of the past were designed for good resonance and unplugged volume, but the ES-175 was manufactured with amplified sound in mind, and its less powerful acoustic tone, combined with the different structural response of laminated wood, made it far less susceptible to feedback, especially with the slightly smaller body size of the 175.

It transpired that this choice not only had no downside but also made it possible to sell the model at a lower price, which came as good news to musicians, who are rarely rolling in cash. The superb guitar shown here dates from 1953, a time when the ES-175 had a single P90 in the neck position. This stellar model went through numerous versions, with twin P90s, followed from 1957 by humbuckers, and always remained one of the brand's bestsellers.

Year of manufacture: 1953
Country: United States
Approximate resale value: £5,800
Hear it on: Pat Metheny, 'Sirabhorn' (1976)

# Martin D-45

**Some models are so rare that most collectors dare not even consider them. Money is obviously a prime factor, but even a fan with bottomless pockets would not necessarily be able to find an example of the most sought-after guitar of all time, the pre-war Martin D-45.**

•

'Pre-war' is a fuzzy term, since the last examples were sold in 1942. The United States had by this time been involved in hostilities for a year, but the Nazareth factory had not ceased operation. Nonetheless, 1942 was the last year of production of the D-45, a Martin model to raise the pulse of every guitarist because of its extreme rarity and undeniable prestige.

The 45 suffix had been a feature of the catalogue since 1904 and the dreadnought shape (invented by another brand in 1915) had been used by Martin since 1931, but it was not until 1933 that a young cowboy ordered the first instrument to combine these two characteristics, creating the first D-45. Gene Autry, the cowboy in question, even asked for his name to inlaid along the fretboard. He was not a real cowboy at all, but rather the most famous 'singing cowboy' on the silver screen of the time, a yodeller from Oklahoma and a true superstar who could easily afford the US$225 that a D-45 cost (twice the price of a D-28 at the time).

The D-45 was highly decorated, with mother-of-pearl binding throughout, hexagonal mother-of-pearl fret markers, gold hardware and a vertical logo borrowed from the brand's archtop models. Few musicians of the era could afford this level of luxury, however, and only 91 such guitars were manufactured between 1933 and 1942.

In the 1960s musicians started taking such a keen interest in these pre-war Martins that some luthiers, among them Mike Longworth from Tennessee, offered the conversion of pre-war D-28s (which did not yet cost as much as a house) into D-45s. Martin thus decided to re-release the model in 1968, and the current models are still fantastic acoustic guitars at the top of the brand's range.

Year of manufacture: 1942
Country: United States
Approximate resale value: £834,100
Hear it on: Gene Autry, 'Back in the Saddle Again' (1939)

# Gretsch
## Country Club

**The Brooklyn brand Gretsch was the last to throw its hat into the ring in the battle of the archtops between Gibson and Epiphone, but it made a very significant contribution. It was none other than Gretsch that hit upon the idea that radically changed the philosophy underlying instruments that tended towards austerity, despite their decoration: the introduction of colour.**

•

The Gibson L-5 and Epiphone Emperor were the benchmark models for the most demanding jazz guitarists of the 1930s, and the quality of Gretsch's response was not really up to scratch, although it should be noted that the brand, which had been founded in 1883, had previously been far more involved in manufacturing drum kits and banjos, along with low-end guitars for other distributors. Its first venture into the world of electric archtops came in 1939, three years after Gibson's ES-150, and it was nothing to strike fear into any heart. The first cutaway models arrived in 1951, however, proof that the Brooklyn factory had no plans to throw in the towel.

It was not until 1954 that Gretsch released its 6196, also called the Country Club, in Cadillac Green. The name Country Club was ambiguous; it was obviously an attempt to court country guitarists, but a country club is primarily a private club reserved for the very rich to indulge in various activities, so the model is more an evocation of luxury. That idea extended to the name of the colour, which was taken directly from the colour library of General Motors. The other available shade, Jaguar Tan, was also taken from the world of cars.

Up to this point, archtops had had ultra-traditional looks, and although the Super 400 and John D'Angelico's guitars were richly decorated with mother-of-pearl, the finishes were restricted to natural or sunburst. With the Country Club, Gretsch moved the guitar world into Technicolor, and nothing would ever be the same again. Jazzers never really embraced this development, but rock guitarists were fascinated by it. In this respect, Gretsch was a true trailblazer, since Fender and Gibson would not develop their custom colour palettes until the 1960s.

Year of manufacture: 1958
Country: United States
Approximate resale value: £5,000
Hear it on: Rancid, 'Fall Back Down' (2003)
Guitarist: Tim Armstrong

GRETSCH
GRETSCH
BY
Bigsby

# Gibson
## Les Paul Gold Top

**The Les Paul is Gibson's iconic shape and one of the most legendary instruments in guitar history, but it started life as the signature model of a jazz star, with a rather adventurous design for its time.**

•

Les Paul was by turns an inventor, sound engineer and renowned guitarist, achieving particular fame for the duo he formed with his wife, Mary Ford. He was also one of the first musicians to be convinced of the virtues of the solid-body guitar (a construction that avoided the feedback problems inherent in hollow instruments), and Gibson eventually decided to give his signature model a go in 1952.

The Kalamazoo brand was a little conservative, and the only electrics in its catalogue were beautiful archtops. The design of the Les Paul was greatly indebted to this mindset, and featured the glued-in neck and carved maple top that meant an archtop could not just be thrown together like a Telecaster.

The first version of the Les Paul was called the Gold Top after the colour of the finish on its front side (the body and the back of the neck had the natural colour of their lacquered mahogany). It came fitted with two single-coil P90 pickups, a model that was already in existence at the brand, but in a new version with a cream-coloured finish and no mounting screws at the sides, nicknamed 'soap bars'. The bridge on the first Les Pauls was a model designed by Paul himself and did not work as well as it might; it was replaced in 1953 by a combined bridge/tailpiece assembly dubbed the 'wraparound'.

There was no overnight success for the Les Paul, since the jazzers at whom it was aimed did not fully grasp the appeal of this new instrument. It was, however, rediscovered by a later generation who appreciated it to the full.

Year of manufacture: 1955
Country: United States
Approximate resale value: £41,700
Hear it on: Sister Rosetta Tharpe, *Gospel Train* (1956)

# Gibson SG Junior

**When the shape of the Les Paul metamorphosed into the SG, the entire range followed suit, from the top-of-the-range Les Paul Custom (which turned white in the process) to the less expensive Les Paul Junior, which gained a little more bite and aggression in its transition.**

•

By 1961 Les Pauls were not selling any more (apart from Junior and Special models), and Gibson decided to alter their shape radically, moving over to two Florentine cutaways for unrestricted access to the high frets, and to the Cherry Red colour that had been featured on the old Les Paul Juniors and Specials since 1958 and was then introduced for the Standard. In 1962 Les Paul declined to renew the contract that had bound him to the Kalamazoo brand for the previous ten years, and Gibson was obliged to come up with another name for this new model, which simply became the SG (solid guitar). It should be noted that the Les Paul was Gibson's first solid-body and, since the brand already had the ES model prefix for hollow-body or semi-hollow electrics, it was only logical to have initials for solid-body guitars as well.

Despite all these changes, the SG Junior remained a guitar of great simplicity, bordering on perfection, with the addition of a thinner chamfered body that gave it an even brighter, clearer sound. The rest – the combination of a mahogany body and neck with a rosewood fretboard, a single P90 and a wraparound bridge – was left untouched, and to this day the SG Junior represents a good way for guitarists looking for a rock 'n' roll machine that does not cost an arm and a leg to get their hands on the Gibson sound. For a model in the rare Polaris White finish shown here, the bill will be a little steeper, of course. Its elder sibling the Special (which sports a neck pickup and more ornate decoration) has been played by Pete Townshend and Tony Iommi. There are worse pedigrees.

Year of manufacture: 1963
Country: United States
Approximate resale value: £5,000
Hear it on: Tom Petty, 'Runnin' Down a Dream' (1989)
Guitarist: Mike Campbell

NORMAL
VOLUME
TREBLE
BASS
VOLUME
TREBLE
BASS
SPEED
INTENSITY
PRESENCE
Fender

# Harmony
# Rocket H54

**Harmony has never been a byword for quality in the same way as the better-known big brands, but, in terms of sheer quantity, no American company manufactured as many guitars as this modest purveyor of cheap instruments from the 1930s to the 1960s.**

•

The roots of Harmony date back to 1882, when German émigré Wilhelm Schultz set up a musical instrument factory employing about 40 people to supply department stores and mail-order catalogues, and it was Sears, Roebuck & Co., the leaders in this very field, that bought Harmony in 1916. It should be noted that the location of the factory in Chicago, on the shores of the Great Lakes and a stone's throw from the Midwest, was perfect to place the brand at the crossroads of postal routes.

By 1930 the brand had sold half a million instruments, including ukuleles, banjos, mandolins and guitars. It regained its independence in 1940 (which is why Sears turned to other suppliers for its Silvertone brand), and in 1965 alone, at the height of the British Invasion, it sold no fewer than 350,000 instruments, mostly guitars.

The models included the Meteor, a hollow quarter-body that was Keith Richards's first electric when the Rolling Stones were getting started in 1963, and the Rocket, which was the same shape but featured a cap in maple rather than spruce, and an unmistakable red finish. Three variations were available: the H53 with a single neck pickup, the twin-pickup H54 (shown here) and the H59 (try to follow the logic…) with three pickups. The pickups in question were made by DeArmond in Ohio, and their golden mesh gave them the generic nickname of 'gold foils'.

Harmony was unfortunately unable to withstand competition from Japanese guitars that were even cheaper to manufacture, and the brand shut up shop in 1975. Nonetheless, the sheer number of guitars it produced should guarantee that many musicians on the lookout for vintage bargains will be able to rediscover them for a while to come.

Year of manufacture: 1966
Country: United States
Approximate resale value: £1,300
Hear it on: The Black Keys, 'Little Black Submarines' (2011)
Guitarist: Dan Auerbach

Two-Rock
PRESENCE
BASS
MIDDLE
TREBLE
VOLUME
INPUTS
VIBRATO
Two-Rock
Harmony
Gibson
IN
OUT
FUZZ
VOLUME
FUZZ
ARBITER · ENGLAND

# Gretsch Billy Bo

**The discreetly retro-futuristic design of the Billy Bo has its own tale to tell and represents a link between three generations of musicians who did not fear to take the road less travelled in their choice of instrument. And the guitar shown here is proof positive that the torch has already been passed on to a fourth generation.**

•

By a quirk of history, the Billy Bo did not start life at Gretsch. The legendary singer and songwriter Bo Diddley was already playing a red Gretsch Duo Jet (technically a Jet Firebird) and had come up with some ideas for fanciful shapes to modify the design of his solid-body guitar from Brooklyn. In 1959 he asked a former employee of the company to make him three guitars, all with a red top, a black body and Filter'Tron pickups (just like the Jet Firebird). These were the rectangular Cigar Box guitar that Gretsch has since reissued; the Cadillac, which got very little play and has not been reproduced to this day; and the Jupiter Thunderbird.

The rest of the story is so garbled that it sounds fabricated, as is invariably the case when the source is ZZ Top guitarist Billy Gibbons, and in this lies its charm. Quite when or why is unknown, but it seems Diddley presented the Jupiter Thunderbird to Gibbons, who kept it in his enormous collection before using it for a recording in the 2000s. It was not until 2005 that Gretsch released the Billy Bo, however, a double signature model linking Diddley and Gibbons, with the original shape but fitted with Power'Tron pickups that are more powerful than the first iteration.

The next generation to take an interest in the model included Jack White, who plumped for a Billy Bo in white (White Falcon-style), both for his duet with Alicia Keys on the original soundtrack of the James Bond film *Quantum of Solace* (2008) and for his Dead Weather outfit. And the latest generation of enthusiasts has already arrived in the form of Henri Cash of Starcrawler, who is the owner of this incredible silver sparkle version with only three strings. The future of rock is in safe hands.

Years of manufacture: 2010s
Country: United States
Approximate resale value: £4,200
Hear it on: Starcrawler, 'I Love LA' (2018)
Guitarist: Henri Cash

GRETSCH
STARCRAWLER
NORMAL
BRIGHT
VOLUME
TREBLE
BASS
VIBRATO
BRIGHT
VOLUME
TREBLE
MIDDLE
BASS
Super Reverb-Amp
FENDER ELECT. INST. CO.
Fender
GRETSCH
BY
Bigsby

**Gretsch Billy Bo**

Gretsch released the first sparkle-finish guitar in history with the Silver Jet of 1955, taking advantage of finishes that had been developed for the brand's drum kits. This fancy detail, which has been used in various ways on a number of models, has become a visual trademark for the brand.

Thanks are due to Anna for her support and enthusiasm, to the team at AllRight for their faith, to Eleanor for her magnificent photos and, above all, to all those whose guitars are featured on these pages:

Mark Agnesi, Shai Ashkenazi, Peredur ap Gwynedd, Dick Boak, Joe Bonamassa, Tyler Bryant, Tom Bukovac, Barrie Cadogan, Christie and Walter Carter, Henri Cash, Christian Earl, John Frusciante, Peter Grønborg Dorvil at Guitar Hunter, Daniel Gallagher, Gary Gand, Cesar Gueikian, Larry Hall, Norman Harris, Richard Head, Luke Hobbs at Gardiner Houlgate, Scott Holiday, Phillip Hylander, Jim Irsay, Martin Kelly, Mike Long at ATB Guitars, Scott McKeon, Bernie Marsden, Greg Martin, Keith Nelson, Niklas Nikolajsen, Giles Palmer, Marc Ransley, Brian Ray, Rob Sampson, John Shanks, John Shults, Steven Solomon, Marty Stuart, Eddie Tatton, Steve Tracy, Chris Turpin, Scott Willis, Bob Wootton and Rick Zsigmond.

Originally published in the French language under the title: *Guitares d'exception*

First published in Great Britain in 2025 by Cassell,
an imprint of Octopus Publishing Group Ltd,
Carmelite House, 50 Victoria Embankment,
London EC4Y 0DZ
www.octopusbooks.co.uk
www.octopusbooksusa.com

An Hachette UK Company
www.hachette.co.uk

The authorized representative in the EEA is Hachette Ireland,
8 Castlecourt Centre, Dublin 15, D15 XTP3, Ireland (email: info@hbgi.ie)

Distributed in the US by Hachette Book Group, 1290 Avenue of the Americas,
4th and 5th Floors, New York, NY 10104

Distributed in Canada by Canadian Manda Group, 664 Annette St, Toronto,
Ontario, Canada M6S 2C8



ISBN 978 1 78840 632 1

A CIP catalogue record for this book is available from the British Library.

Printed in China

1 3 5 7 9 10 8 6 4 2

Publisher: Trevor Davies
Project Editor: Faye Robson
English translation by JMS Books LLP
Copy Editor: Rosanna Fairhead
Creative Director: Jonathan Christie
Designer: Jeremy Tilston
Production Manager: Caroline Alberti

Publisher's note
All prices and resale valuations were correct at the time of writing in 2020 and have been converted
to GBP as required. Current prices and resale values may have changed since first publication.
Neither the publisher nor the author can accept any liability for any financial or other loss incurred
by reliance placed on the information contained in this book.